The Backward Step

Other Books by Ben Howard

POETRY

Leaf, Sunlight, Asphalt
(Salmon Poetry, 2009)

Dark Pool
(Salmon Poetry, 2004)

Midcentury
(Salmon Poetry, 1997)

Lenten Anniversaries: Poems 1982–1989
(The Cummington Press, 1990)

Northern Interior: Poems 1975–1982
(The Cummington Press, 1986)

Father of Waters: Poems 1965–1976
(Abattoir Editions: University of Nebraska at Omaha, 1979)

PROSE

Entering Zen
(Whitlock Publishing, 2011)

The Pressed Melodeon: Essays on Modern Irish Writing
(Story Line Press, 1996)

The Backward Step

Ben Howard

WHITLOCK PUBLISHING
ALFRED, NY

The Backward Step by Ben Howard

First Whitlock Publishing edition 2014

Whitlock Publishing
P.O. Box 472
Alfred, NY 14802

Copyright © Ben Howard 2014

ISBN 10: 0-9770956-1-4
ISBN 13: 978-0-9770956-1-2

This book was set in Dante on 55# acid-free paper that meets ANSI standards for archival quality.

Printed in the United States of America.

For Robin

Contents

Preface	xi
Ordinary Mind	1
Near and Far	5
The Harp of Myanmar	9
Mishaps and Mistakes	13
Rest-Stroke, Free-Stroke	17
Flappers	21
One Thing at a Time	25
Gardens of Fear and Desire	29
Just Say "Oops!"	33
Contenders	37
An Appropriate Response	41
The Backward Step	45
Inhabiting Zen	49
A Life's Work	53
Being Positive	56
In the Waiting Room	60
The Music of What Happens	64
Dramatis Personae	68
Contemplative Memory	72
The Virtues of Solitude	76
The Elbow Does Not Bend Outward	80
Fresh Listening	84
The Practice of Peace	88
Seventy Percent	92
Paying Heed	96

The Ego Filter	100
Consistency	104
Quiet Persistence	108
Wait Up!	112
Timeless Flowers	116
Fixed Ideas	121
Watch What You're Doing	125
Mudita and Social Media	129
The Cliché Monster	133
Just Say "Oh"	137
Noble Silence	141
This World Uncertain Is	145
True Equanimity	149
Resting in the Immediate	153
This Is, Because That Is	157
Dropping and Adding	161
Taking Care of Our Lives	165
Realizing	169
The Handwritten Word	173
Wise Attention	177
Snow	181
Unwelcome Sounds	185
Past and Present	189
Cooked Carrots	193
Elsewhere	196
Notes	200
About the Author	213

Preface

Zen meditation is a simple practice. With proper instruction, anyone can do it. As a daily discipline, however, Zen practice is difficult to sustain. Hectic everyday life assumes the foreground, and practice gets pushed to the side.

That need not be so. The Buddha's Way is endless, the fourth Great Vow informs us, and for monastics and lay practitioners alike, the integration of Zen practice into ordinary life can become a joyful, lifelong challenge. In Buddhist teachings, that challenge is often likened to cultivating a garden. Nutrients are required, as is an attitude of careful attention.

In *Entering Zen*, my previous collection of essays, I endeavored to introduce the fundamentals of Zen practice and the leading themes of the Zen tradition. In the present essays, I have continued that effort, addressing my comments to beginners as well as seasoned practitioners. At the same time, I have focused less on explaining Zen practice than on exploring ways of *inhabiting* it: of allowing its benign influence to permeate every dimension of one's life and every cell of one's being.

That effort can begin with what Zen Master Eihei Dogen (1200-1253) called "the backward step." "Stop searching for phrases and chasing after words," wrote Dogen Zenji. "Take the backward step and turn the light inward." Revered in the Soto Zen tradition, Dogen's words remind us that at any moment we can halt our headlong rush into the future. We can awaken from our dream-world and return to the reality of the present moment. And, in Dogen's famous phrase, we can "drop off body and mind," shifting our orientation from egocentric thinking to selfless awareness. By so doing, we can live in greater freedom and forestall harm to ourselves and others.

Dogen Zenji is one of the many Zen teachers quoted in these essays. Although Zen masters admonish us to rely, first and last, upon our own experience, I am indebted to the Venerable Thich Nhat Hanh, Shinge Roko Sherry Chayat Roshi, Roshi Joan Halifax, Zoketsu Norman Fischer, and the other teachers cited in this collection. Their insights have guided my practice and deepened my understanding of Zen. No less important, I am grateful to my readers, local and worldwide, whose responses have supported and helped to shape this continuing project. Thanks also to David Snyder, editor of the community newspaper *The Alfred Sun*, in whose pages these biweekly essays first appeared, and to Allen Grove, director of Whitlock Publishing, who has provided these fugitive writings with a handsome and enduring home. And special thanks to my wife,

Robin, my first and most steadfast reader, who has patiently companioned my search for phrases and my unregenerate chasing after words.

—Ben Howard
Alfred, New York
July, 2013

Ordinary Mind

It's winter in Western New York, and this morning our driveway is filled with new-fallen snow. As I look out at that white expanse, I am reminded of a poem by Billy Collins, poet of American domestic life.

Entitled "Shoveling Snow with Buddha," Collins' poem depicts two men at work in a snow-filled driveway. One is the narrator, who might be Everyman—or at least every man who owns a home and lives in a northern climate. The other is the Buddha, who, as the narrator observes, is out of his customary habitat:

> *In the usual iconography of the temple or the local Wok*
> *you would never see him doing such a thing,*
> *tossing the dry snow over the mountain*
> *of his bare, round shoulder,*
> *his hair tied in a knot,*
> *a model of concentration.*
>
> *- - -*

Even the season is wrong for him.
In all his manifestations, is it not warm and slightly humid?
Is this not implied by his serene expression,
that smile so wide it wraps itself around the waist of the universe?

Unlikely workmates, one might say. And though the two are toiling harmoniously together, they appear to have little in common. With every heave of snow, the narrator notes, they become "lost to each other / in these sudden clouds of [their] own making, / these fountain-bursts of snow." And even when they are visible to each other, their ways of working set them apart.

The narrator, one infers, is a good-natured, affable fellow. He enjoys the outdoors, and even though his present chore will consume the better part of the morning, he doesn't mind. He is also a talkative, opinionated soul, who likens shoveling snow to a religious experience. "This is so much better than a sermon in church," he declares. "This is the true religion, the religion of snow, / and sunlight and winter geese barking in the sky." Perhaps it is Sunday morning, and he is playing hooky. In any event, he rattles on, offering a running commentary on his experience.

The Buddha, however, is too absorbed to listen:

He has thrown himself into shoveling snow
as if it were the purpose of existence,
as if the sign of a perfect life were a clear driveway
you could back the car down easily
and drive off into the vanities of the world
with a broken heater fan and a song on the radio.

In contrast to the narrator, who stands at a remove from his task and can't stop talking, the Buddha labors "inside the generous pocket of his silence," immersed in the work at hand. In the language of Zen, he is in a state of *samadhi*, or one-pointed concentration. He is performing *samu*, or silent work practice, an integral component of Zen meditation. And as he "drives the thin blade again / deep into the glittering white snow," he exemplifies the state of *muga*, in which the duality of self and other dissolves, and subject and object become one. For those in that state, commentary becomes superfluous and personal views extraneous. One does what must be done.

Given their differences, the narrator and the Buddha might seem to inhabit two different worlds. The narrator embodies what Zen calls "ordinary," discriminating mind, which engages in such activities as comparing two religions and judging one superior to the other. Conversing incessantly with itself, that mind also speaks out loud, offering its views and judgments to whoever will listen. By contrast, the Buddha exemplifies "Buddha mind," which is silent, open, and grounded in interdependent reality. If the Buddha's mind resembles a freshly cleared driveway, the narrator's resembles the car with its broken heater fan, navigating the vanities of the world.

Yet, according to classical Zen teachings, ordinary mind and Buddha mind are not two separate things. The one depends on the other. In Billy Collins's poem, this interpenetration is dramatized in a surprising moment, when the Buddha suddenly breaks his silence and steps, as it were, out of character:

After this, he asks,
can we go inside and play cards?

Certainly, I reply, and I will heat some milk
and bring cups of hot chocolate to the table
while you shuffle the deck,
and our boots stand dripping by the door.

In this brief exchange, apparent opposites are reconciled: outdoors and indoors, coldness and warmth, work and play, ordinary mind and Buddha mind. The exotic Eastern image of the Buddha merges with the Western domestic world of cards, hot chocolate, and dripping boots.

Ordinary mind is the Buddha mind. Everyday mind is the Way. Attributed to the Ch'an master Mazu Daoji (709-788), these familiar Zen sayings point toward the co-existence, in the midst of any human activity, of rational thought and transcendent awareness: of the ordinary, ego-driven mind and a deeper, intuitive awareness of interdependent reality. If the first mind compares, evaluates, chatters, and keeps track of time, the second forgets itself in whatever it is doing, becoming a silent, egoless part of the stream of life. To view ordinary mind in the perspective of Buddha mind is a central aim of Zen practice. And Billy Collins's lovely poem, however fanciful its imagery or playful its tone, demonstrates a clear understanding of that challenge.

10 February 2011

Near and Far

Twenty-five years ago, Markus Koch was a defensive lineman for the Washington Redskins. During his third season, he broke his lumbar vertebrae, but he continued to play for three more years. Now in his late forties, he suffers from depression, and when he stands for extended periods of time, his legs go numb.

Recently, Markus Koch reflected on the gap between football fans watching the game at home and the physical experience of the players on the field. To close that gap, he facetiously suggested, players might be fitted with a mouth guard that "registers the impact they're getting on the field, and at certain g-forces the helmet shell would crack and explode and leak gray matter and blood." Or, conversely, the fan might be fitted with an adjustable pneumatic suit, which would be "telemetrically linked to a player on the field." In that way the fan could "experience what the player is going through."

Markus Koch's suggestions, quoted by Ben McGrath in his article "Does Football Have a Future?", illustrate what

McGrath calls the "necessary abstraction that allows fans to view their football heroes as characters rather than as people with families." Although McGrath's subject is professional football, the "necessary abstraction" to which he refers is hardly limited to football-watching or even to the world of sports. Truth be told, we create abstractions whenever we watch TV, whether the figures on the screen be football players, celebrities, or the protesters in Cairo. Viewing other people through the lens of the broadcast media, we tend to make characters of them all. And even when we view them "up close and personal," what we are encountering is not so much their personal experience as their assigned roles and their edited personae, accompanied by a reporter's interpretive commentary. As the social critic Frank Rich recently noted, when watching the demonstrations in Cairo, we are "more likely to hear speculation about how many cents per gallon the day's events might cost at the pump than to get an intimate look at the demonstrators' lives."

To be sure, we can always turn off our TVs. But should we do so, and should we become cognizant of what is unfolding within and around us, we may find that the habit of objectifying the "other" persists in our private reflections, even when the other is ourselves. We, too, create necessary abstractions. We, too, mediate, mainly by means of images and concepts, between our minds and our ever-changing lives. And, as the Vipassana teacher Jack Kornfield once observed, what we know of ourselves is often what we *think* about ourselves. Or what others think. Or some amalgam of the two.

By way of illustration, please take a few minutes to describe yourself. Imagine yourself to be a separate, solid entity, and describe your most salient features. Those features might include your physical attributes, your temperament, your interests, your social and professional roles, and your family relationships. Consider others' perceptions as well as your own.

Now set your description aside. Sit in an upright, stable, and balanced posture. Follow your breathing for a minute or two. Then do nothing but be aware of whatever is happening in your body, your surroundings, and your state of mind. If a sound occurs, take note of it; if your back hurts, be present for the pain; if a thought comes along, acknowledge it; if you grow impatient, bored, or judgmental, recognize those passing mental states.

When you have sat in this way for ten minutes or so, stop and examine what has just occurred. Compare your self-description with the evidence of your senses. What, if anything, do these modes of inquiry have in common? What kinds of knowledge does each of them provide? To what degree and in what ways was your description verified by your experience? To what extent was your experience encompassed by your description?

To propose this experiment is not to suggest that descriptions are always false or that experience, as the saying goes, is the true and only teacher. Rather, it is to illuminate the choice we have at any given moment. We can draw back, making solid objects of our "selves," our experiences, and other people. Employing images, concepts, and other vehicles of abstraction, we can make characters of ourselves and stories of our experiences. We can entertain ourselves, while also reinforcing our sense of separation.

But at any moment we can also draw near, both to ourselves and to the world. Rather than cling to our personal stories, we can become fully aware of our moment-to-moment lives, just as they are. Rather than adhere to habits of thought and feeling, we can fully experience our experience, however pleasant or unpleasant, comforting or troubling it may be. And rather than objectify the protester in Tahrir Square or the linebacker incurring a life-altering injury, we can cultivate our connection to others' suffering.

24 February 2011

The Harp of Myanmar

As the world knows, Aung San Suu Kyi, the Nobel peace prize laureate and leader of the opposition in Myanmar, was released from house arrest in November, 2010. What is not so well known is that during her long years of confinement—fifteen of the past twenty-one—Aung San Suu Kyi relied on meditation to maintain her equanimity. Every morning, she practiced Vipassana ("insight") meditation, concentrating on the rising and falling of her abdomen. Her practice, she has since reported, enabled her to deal with the "intense irritation and impatience" she felt toward those who had imprisoned her. It also helped her cope with the loss of her husband to prostate cancer and her subsequent estrangement from her two sons. "After years of meditation," she has said, "I think you remain very much on an even keel. There is not much difference to you mentally whether you've been released or not."

Myanmar used to be called Burma. And Aung San Suu Kyi's meditative stability in the midst of political turmoil brings to mind Michio Takeyama's novel *Harp of Burma*

(1946), whose central theme is the preservation of one's humanity in a time of war. Set in the last days of World War II and the period immediately following, this short novel depicts a company of war-weary Japanese soldiers, who are losing their campaign against the British in the tropical jungles of Burma. Fortunately for the troops, their captain is a musician, who has taught the men to sing; and though they are exhausted and homesick, they have kept their spirits up by singing Western and Japanese songs. Among their favorites is "Hanyu no Yado," a Japanese version of "Home, Sweet Home." And in one of the most memorable scenes in the novel, in which the company is surrounded by British forces and is bracing itself for an attack, the company's harpist, Corporal Mizushima, plays "Hanyu no Yado" on his Burmese harp. To everyone's surprise, the British soldiers hidden in the forest can be heard singing "Home, Sweet Home." Shortly thereafter, the British come out of hiding, and the Japanese learn that the war is over.

In that pivotal scene, Corporal Mizushima assumes the foreground. And as the novel progresses, Mizushima's personal transformation becomes the center of attention. A man of meditative disposition, whose face wears "the sad, contemplative expression that tropical peoples such as the Burmese often have," he is sent on a mission to persuade a remnant of Japanese troops, who are holding out against British artillery, to give up their suicidal effort and surrender. His mission fails, and he is separated from his company. To survive, he acquires a monk's robes and wanders unnoticed through the villages. But as the narrator observes, clothes influence a person's outlook; and it is not long before Mizushima, who has been impersonating a Theravadan Buddhist monk, elects to become one. Wearing his robes, he visits the British prison camp where his fellow soldiers have been confined, and they observe that he "seems to be meditating, peering into his own heart." Later they learn that Mizushima, having come upon the decomposing bodies of Japanese soldiers during his wanderings, has decided to stay in Burma to bury the dead.

Throughout *Harp of Burma*, Mizushima's peaceful, meditative temperament is associated with the 13-string Burmese harp, an ancient instrument with a long and venerable tradition. Made of "finely polished inlaid wood and shaped like an eggplant," it produces a lingering, ethereal sound. As the narrator explains, Burmese music is said to have begun in imitation of rain drops, and the tones of the Burmese harp, "now high, now low," are "joined in innumerable intertwining strands, falling in and out like the long sigh of a soul drifting toward heaven." By its very nature, the Burmese harp induces a sense of peace. And in *Harp of Burma*, the instrument's gentle tones, rooted in nature and harmonious with natural rhythms, come to represent a way of being that Takeyama attributes to the Burmese people. In contrast to the overweening Japanese, the Burmese "accept the world as it is," rather than try "to change it according to their own designs." Rather than "wishing to master everything through strength or intellect," they "aim for salvation through humility and reliance on a power greater than themselves." Rather than try "to control nature by their efforts," they have learned to "yield to it and merge into a broader, deeper order of being."

Sixty years on, Takeyama's vision of Burmese culture may seem as dated as it is idealized. The Buddhist monks who protested against the military dictatorship in September, 2007 were not accepting the world as it is, and in the junta's brutal response there was not the least sign of yielding. But a suggestive and heartening continuity may be found between the fictional character Mizushima, whose evolving meditative awareness engenders compassionate action, and the real-life presence of Aung San Suu Kyi, whose constructive, courageous leadership has been supported by meditative practice.

9 March 2011

Mishaps and Mistakes

If you have lived in a northern climate for any length of time, the chances are good that you have slipped and fallen on an icy sidewalk. Or that you will, no matter how careful you are.

Such was the case a few weeks back, as I was walking down the sidewalk in Alfred, New York, wearing shoes more suitable to spring than winter. Coming upon a puddle in the middle of the sidewalk, I stepped onto a mound of ice to avoid the water. Down I went, face forward, landing on my knee.

Thanks, I suspect, to my daily practice of T'ai Chi, I was back on my feet a moment later, suffering no worse injury than a scraped knee. But as the day wore on, and as I felt the lasting effects of my fall, I considered what to call it. Was it a *mishap*—something, as they used to say in Ireland, that could happen to a bishop? Or was it an avoidable *mistake*? Although those two small words share a common prefix, their meanings differ widely, as do their implications.

The word mishap derives from the root *hap*, which means "chance" or "luck." From the same root come *happiness, perhaps*, and *happenstance*. *Hap* was once an English word, as can be seen in Thomas Hardy's sonnet by that name, in which the poet ponders the causes of his misery. After entertaining the possibility that he is being punished by a vengeful deity, he concludes that the operative force is "Crass Casualty," Hardy's synonym for chance, or "hap," or the luck of the draw. Nowadays, *hap* is archaic, but its meaning survives in the word mishap, which the *O.E.D.* defines as "an unlucky accident." As late as the nineteenth century, *mishap* was also a polite term for a "fall from chastity," as in "In her youth, Lady Betty made a mishap."

Mistake is of another order entirely, mainly because it involves human volition. Derived from a root meaning "to grasp" or "to understand," the word mistake may refer to a conceptual error. At any time, any one of us may be *mistaken*. We may fail to "take" another person's meaning. More often, however, the word mistake refers to an action, such as swerving out of one's lane while driving, a move that the National Highway Traffic Safety Administration has identified as the leading cause of lethal crashes. Cars do not drive themselves, at least not yet. When a traffic accident occurs, almost always someone has made a mistake.

Eihei Dogen Zenji (1200-1253), founder of the Soto school of Zen, famously described a Zen master's life as "one continuous mistake." *Shoshaku jushaku*, the phrase he used, means "to succeed wrong with wrong." Hearing that phrase, I'm reminded of Roy, a friend from my high-school days, who tried three times before passing his driving test. Not long afterward, Roy was ticketed for speeding on a road at the edge of town. And not long after that, he was ticketed again by the same cop on the same road and lost his hard-earned driver's license. Up to that point at least, Roy's life was indeed one continuous mistake.

And yet in fairness to Dogen Zenji as well as to Roy, we may recall that most mistakes have many mothers and fathers. One of the cardinal tenets of Zen teachings, a principle known as "dependent co-origination," states that in ultimate reality, everything depends upon everything else. Things that we conventionally regard as solid and separate are, in reality, constantly changing, and they have no inherent existence. Nor do they arise, *ex nihilo*, from nowhere. Rather, they arise from concrete causes and conditions, as do we ourselves. We too are constantly being created and re-created by causes and conditions, and like our so-called successes and failures, our mistakes are not simply the results of our personal volitions. They are also expressions of our conditioning, cultural and personal, and their roots may lie as much in our ancestry as in our conscious choices. Like the farmer in Robert Frost's poem "Mending Wall," who quotes the adage "good fences make good neighbors" and "will not go beyond his father's saying," we too can become prisoners of our cultural and familial conditioning.

Lady Betty made a mishap: that archaic usage, so foreign to a contemporary ear, suggests that at one time the distinction between a mishap and a mistake was not so clearly drawn. And in the light of historical, intergenerational interdependence, what appear to be mishaps may be seen as the consequences of long-forgotten mistakes, such as that of situating a major American city on a flood plain. To cultivate awareness of such connectedness may not prevent our everyday mishaps, our slips on the ice or dropping of car keys in the snow. But over time it can help to forestall our most grievous future mistakes. To borrow Abraham Lincoln's resonant phrase, it can help us to know where we are, and whither we are tending.

24 March 2011

Rest-Stroke, Free-Stroke

"The song of the piano," wrote the Catalan poet Eugenio d'Ors, "is a discourse. The song of the cello is an elegy. The song of the guitar . . . is a song."

Those well-known lines, which please guitarists but tend to annoy pianists and cellists, suggest that the song of the guitar is as natural as that of one's favorite bird. The Carolina Wren, perhaps, or the Hermit Thrush. That may well be true, but the production of the guitar's seemingly natural song requires the mastery of two basic right-hand strokes, known to classical guitarists as *apoyando* and *tirando*. These two strokes produce two, very different timbres. And they also exemplify two different ways of paying attention.

In English, *apoyando* is known as the "rest-stroke." The technique takes its name from the fact that when the player's fingertip has executed the stroke, it comes to rest on the adjacent string. But as my friend and fellow guitarist Moises Guevara explained to me, in Spanish the infinitive *apoyar* ("to rest"), from which *apoyando* is derived, also means "to press."

That meaning accords with the stroke itself, in which the player presses the string downward in the direction of the soundboard. This vertical action causes the soundboard to resonate, producing a deep, round tone.

In contrast to *apoyando*, the *tirando* stroke produces a thinner, brighter sound, in which the overtones are as prominent as the fundamental tone. In Spanish, *tirando* means "pulling," but in relation to the guitar the term is conventionally translated as "free-stroke." Executing the free-stroke, the player's fingernail pulls the string in a horizontal direction, passing freely above the adjacent strings. As might be expected, guitarists routinely use the free-stroke for arpeggiated chords, because this stroke allows notes previously played to continue to sound. Correspondingly, the rest-stroke is often used when playing scales and runs. Not only does the stroke produce a strong, clean run. When the scale is ascending, the rest-stroke also silences previous notes and prevents unwelcome dissonance.

Rest-stroke and free-stroke are two, proven means of producing sonorous tones. At the same time, these strokes represent two contrasting ways of bringing attention to bear upon its object. Beyond the context of guitar-playing, these ways of attending may be applied to other activities, including Zen meditation, where paying attention is, as it were, the name of the game. In particular, they may be applied to the practices of conscious breathing and "deep listening."

In the practice of Zen, conscious breathing is both a beginner's first assignment and a seasoned practitioner's abiding task. There are, however, many ways to attend to the breath. One traditional way is to bring concentrated attention to the out-breath while inwardly counting "one," "two," "three," and so on. At the end of each out-breath, we rest in the interval before the next inhalation. Roughly analogous to the rest-stroke, this practice calms the body and concentrates the mind. It is well suited to the beginning of a sitting, especially if one's mind is restless.

As an alternative, however, we can follow the entire cycle of inhalation and exhalation, noting the point where the one turns into the other. Lightly but precisely, we can "tag" that point with a name or number ("out," "one"), while allowing the breath to flow out freely. Analogous to the free-stroke in guitar-playing, this practice sorts well with the later stages of a sitting, when mind and body are already settled, and the intention is not so much to regulate the breath as to become aware of whatever is naturally unfolding, within and without.

The methods of rest- and free-stroke may also be applied to the meditative practice of "deep listening," which is to say, of listening with full attention and a non-judgmental attitude. Engaged in a one-to-one conversation, we can choose to "press" our interlocutor, asking question after question, as we probe the issue at hand. Alternatively, we can simply pose a question or make a suggestion, giving close but relaxed attention to the other person's response. These two ways of listening, analogous respectively to *apoyando* and *tirando*, can be used with discretion and in accordance with the situation. If the first seeks to get to the heart of the matter, the second permits the truth to emerge of its own accord.

When I was first learning to play the guitar, some forty years ago, the rest-stroke was considered primary. The free-stroke was reserved mainly for arpeggios. Nowadays, the free-stroke is considered primary, the rest-stroke being used mainly for accenting a note or passage or creating a dominant melody line. For my own part, however, I've come to use the two strokes circumstantially and in equal measure. And insofar as I can, I do the equivalent when sitting in *zazen*, or engaging in conversation, or going about my daily round. For in everyday life, as in playing the guitar, there are points when it is best to press, or to rest, or, in the words of Shunryu Suzuki Roshi, to let everything go as it goes.

7 April 2011

Flappers

In "A Voyage to Laputa," the third book of *Gulliver's Travels*, Gulliver visits a flying island where the inhabitants "of better quality" are so preoccupied with their thoughts that they fail to take notice of their surroundings. To remedy that situation, each such inhabitant has been supplied with a "Flapper," who carries a "blown bladder fastened like a flail to the end of a short stick." With this device, the Flappers bring their masters' wandering minds back to reality:

> *The Flapper is likewise employed diligently to attend his master in his walks, and upon occasion to give him a soft flap on his eyes, because he is always so wrapped up in cogitation, that he is in manifest danger of falling down every precipice, and bouncing his head against every post, and in the streets, of jostling others, or being jostled himself into the kennel.*

These same dreamers also "forget what they [are] about," until their memories are "roused by their Flappers."

If you are married, as I am, your First Flapper may be your spouse. Who else will tell you that your button-down collar is unbuttoned, or that you are wearing a black belt with brown shoes, or that you have just said something uncommonly silly? Help may also come from a candid friend, who duly notes your slips of the tongue, or from the driver behind you, whose rude horn informs you that the light has changed. But a host of Flappers may also be found in the Zen tradition, which aims to waken us from our daydreams and haul us back to the here and now. Over the centuries, Zen teachers and zendo officers have employed a variety of means toward that end, including shouts, slaps, and robust whacks with the *keisaku* ("encouragement stick"). But for the lay practitioner, who may not be interested in monastic training but would like to lead an awakened life, gentler methods are available. Practiced with diligence, these methods can be as efficacious as a master's barked rebuke or *a keisaku* landing on tender shoulders.

One such method is the *gatha*, or meditative verse, which may be recited before an action is taken. In his book *Present Moment, Wonderful Moment*, Zen master Thich Nhat Hanh offers a variety of *gathas*, traditional and contemporary, to sustain the practice of mindfulness in everyday life:

> *Waking up this morning, I smile.*
> *Twenty-four brand-new hours are before me.*
> *I vow to live fully in each moment*
> *and to look at all beings with eyes of compassion.*
>
> - — -
>
> *In this food,*
> *I see clearly the presence*
> *of the entire universe*
> *supporting my existence.*

Memorized and recited throughout the day, verses such as these heighten our awareness of our often habitual actions. "As exercises in both meditation and poetry," writes Thich Nhat Hanh, "gathas are very much in keeping with the Zen tradition."

A second method, also developed by Thich Nhat Hanh, is known as the "mindfulness bell." Analogous to the actual bell that initiates a period of meditation, the mindfulness bell may be anything regularly encountered in one's daily round—the screen of a cell phone, for example, or the handle of a coffee mug. Like the mezuzah mounted on the door frame of a Jewish home, the objects we have chosen call us back to ourselves, while also reminding us of the preciousness of life, which we honor by being fully present. Thich Nhat Hanh recommends that upon encountering our bells of mindfulness, we stop and take three conscious breaths. In that way we are awakened, time and again, and restored to the present moment.

A third and more demanding method is to ask a friend or family member to monitor our mindfulness. In his book *Being Upright*, Tenshin Reb Anderson recalls a woman who told him that she was doing whatever she was doing "wholeheartedly, with complete awareness." In response he asked her, "How do you know that you are not just dreaming that you are doing whatever you are doing wholeheartedly, with complete awareness?" Developing his point, he asks all of us how we know that we are "not just practicing according to [our] dispositions and going along with [our] prejudices?" And in tandem with these questions, he suggests that "we all need someone in our lives to whom we are accountable, someone whom we have asked to give us feedback on our practice, someone to guide us in finding a balance in the midst of our likes and dislikes." Such a person may be difficult to find—and even more difficult to retain. But practical arrangements can be made, as can reciprocal agreements.

Ideally, the serious practitioner may also find—or endeavor to create—a community of fellow practitioners, known in Zen as a *sangha*. Such a community can not only structure and sustain its participants' individual practice, which in the absence of communal support can quickly fade. Like a conclave of Flappers, the sangha can also keep its members fully awake.

21 April 2011

One Thing at a Time

One thing at a time, Bud, my father used to say. For centuries, Zen teachers have said the same. Whatever you are doing, give that one thing your full attention. *When you walk, just walk.*

That is sound advice, but in our present culture it stands little chance of being heeded. A recent *New Yorker* cartoon depicts an urban couple at an intersection of trails in a state park. While the man studies the printed guide, his companion turns to a passing hiker for help. "Which trail," she asks, "has the best cell-phone reception?" When you walk, just walk, our culture seems to be saying, but keep your cell phone on. Within this prevailing social ethos, the admonition to do one thing at a time, and to give that one thing sustained attention, comes to look like a quaintly archaic notion.

Zen meditation is sometimes viewed as a countervailing force—a potent corrective to so-called multi-tasking. That view is not without an empirical basis: by taking up Zen, people do become more "focused" and less prone to distraction. But in the broader context of the Buddhist tradition, of which Zen is a late flowering, concentrative meditation, or *samatha*, is but one of two general aspects of meditative practice, the other being *vipassana*, or the cultivation of insight into the nature of reality. Each aspect serves the other. And to emphasize one over the other is often to lose sight of the larger aims of Zen discipline.

In Zen training, we do indeed learn to do one thing at a time, silently and wholeheartedly. Concomitantly, we also cultivate an attitude of respect toward all things, including the inanimate objects we encounter in everyday life. Tenshin Reb Anderson, a Soto Zen priest, describes that attitude in this way:

> *In this practice we refrain from handling things carelessly, noisily, or needlessly. All things are treated with the utmost respect. Light and inexpensive things are picked up as if they were heavy and precious. Doors are opened and closed quietly and gently. Our actions are performed in such a manner as to be pleasant and inspiring to all others, animate and inanimate: gentle and encouraging to the door, and kind and careful toward our sitting cushion.*

Paying respectful attention to the smallest thing, we avoid doing harm, while also strengthening our powers of concentration.

Those are laudable objectives, but the practice of "taking care" must itself be handled with care, especially by beginners, lest it subvert the deeper purposes of Zen practice. As the Zen-trained teacher Toni Packer has pointed out, any new skill "can serve as a fresh opportunity to win approval and avoid blame," and being respectfully attentive "can become a self-centered activity that is cultivated because we think it is meritorious in the eyes of others." Being gentle with doors and kind toward our cushions can become a form of conspicuous, self-conscious "mindfulness," rather than selfless immersion in the task at hand.

Beyond the inadvertent reinforcement of egoistic thinking, doing "one thing at a time" can also undermine our social awareness. Toni Packer tells the story of a man at a retreat who stood in a line, slowly and carefully buttoning his cardigan, while failing to notice that people were piling up behind him. During sessions of the Falling Leaf Sangha, our local practice group, I have witnessed similar behavior. In one instance, a young man new to Zen practiced walking meditation at a snail's pace, not realizing that the line was stalled behind him. In another, a practitioner mindfully savored her tea, not noticing that everyone else had finished and was waiting for her to do the same. By their nature concentrative practices exclude other objects of attention, and what is excluded may be the presence of other people.

Such exclusion is awkward for all concerned, and it is also at odds with a central purpose of Zen practice, namely to recognize our interdependence with other beings and to act in accordance with that recognition. In formal Japanese Zen, practitioners endeavor to act in concert, whether the activity be drinking tea or eating a formal (*oryoki*) meal. Although such practice is in part an expression of collective values, it serves primarily to support our awareness of interdependence. When we practice *zazen*, writes Shohaku Okumura, we "settle down peacefully within the network of interdependent origination and allow the universal life force to practice *through us* for all beings." Paying due attention to others in our immediate environment, we continue to cultivate awareness of all sentient beings in their interdependent relationships.

That may sound like the opposite of doing one thing. But paradoxically, by attending to the many we also attend to the One: the timeless, dynamic totality of the web of life. Sometimes called enlightenment, or more modestly, full awakening, that state of awareness cannot be willed into existence. But we can prepare for it, and create propitious conditions for its occurrence, by giving steady, uncompromised attention to one thing at a time.

5 May 2011

Gardens of Fear and Desire

Whatever else it has come to mean, at its root the word meditation means "mental cultivation." To meditate is to cultivate the mind. In contemporary practice, meditation is often a form of awareness training, in which we learn to calm the body, quiet the mind, and bring relaxed attention to the present moment. But Buddhist meditation is also a practice of cultivating certain qualities of mind and heart. At any given moment, the teachings tell us, we are cultivating one thing or another. What we are cultivating may be loving-kindness, compassion, or other "wholesome" states of mind. But it may also be such "unwholesome" states as fear, rage, and the impulse toward destruction.

I was reminded of these teachings while reading *Townie*, an engrossing new memoir by the novelist Andre Dubus III, author of *House of Sand and Fog*. Set in a decaying mill town in the Merrimack Valley, *Townie* depicts a social environment plagued by poverty, alcohol, drugs, violence, and rampant despair. Similar in tone and setting to the film *The Fighter*, the memoir tells a somewhat similar story: that of a bookish, sensitive lad, a "boy easily stomped," who learns how to deal with the local thugs who beat up his brother, call his beautiful mother ugly names, and terrorize anyone weaker than themselves. Driven by his fear, his loathing of bullies, and his desire for connection with his absent father, the "weak little boy" transforms himself by lifting weights and learning how to fight, only to discover, in later years, the deep flaws in what he has wrought. Grounded in a dangerous and rather insular social reality, *Townie* is a tale of willful self-creation and eventual self-discovery. At its most reflective moments, it is also a mature meditation on social injustice, "all the cruelty down through the ages," and the human suffering that engenders brutal acts of violence.

It is not uncommon for weaklings to take up weight-lifting, but in Dubus's case the effort and the product far surpassed the norm. Shamed and humiliated by his tormentors, Dubus resolved to remake himself and become someone so formidable that "no one would even think of trying to hurt [him] or anyone [he] loved." Devoting himself to lifting and later to boxing, he became a defender of the weak and a scourge of the town's drunken, violent louts. By the time he reached his majority, he had hospitalized two such men, one of whom had pushed his brother down a flight of stairs. He had taught himself how to "hurt even more the one you've already hurt." And to bring himself to do such things, he had learned how to break what he calls the "invisible membrane" that surrounds another person's body. To puncture that membrane, he explains, you had to "smash through your own first, your own compassion for another, your own humanity."

For a time, Dubus's self-creation served him well. It enabled him to survive in his culture. As he grew older, however, he came to realize that his rage and his impulse to violence were out of his control. He was becoming a "runaway train," a person from whom he felt profoundly estranged. Concurrent with these realizations, he was also discovering his gifts as a writer. The eldest son of Andres Dubus II, the celebrated American short-story writer, Andres III found joy and release in his father's vocation. By "escaping to the dream on the page," he became more fully present in his own life. Through the contemplative act of writing he discovered ways to "see" rather than worry about being "seen," to listen rather than talk, and to wait rather than attack. Having spent much of his life "making [himself] into a man who did not flee," he learned to peel away the layers of conditioning he had so arduously acquired. In so doing, he discovered a new "membrane," the "one between what we think and what we see, what we believe and what *is*." And to penetrate that membrane, not by physical force but by the power of contemplative insight and the medium of the written word, became his life's work. Having belatedly experienced the power of empathy and the practice of reconciliation, he also discovered ways to alleviate others' suffering

Andres Dubus III's story is as revealing as it is inspiring, not least because it verifies, in contemporary terms, the ancient teaching known as the Four Great Efforts. Simply put, the First and Second Efforts concern unwholesome mental qualities, such as fear and anger, which may or may not have arisen in our psyches. In either case, we give them no nourishment. The Third and Fourth Efforts concern wholesome qualities, such as compassion and equanimity, which have yet to arise or have already arisen. These qualities we develop through meditation. Underlying all four Efforts is the practice of mental cultivation, a process in which we can be consciously and actively involved. As *Townie* so vividly illustrates, we reap what we have sown. We become what we have chosen.

19 May 2011

Just Say "Oops!"

"Whoops!" wrote a friend the other day, having just sent me an e-mail message intended for someone else. Studying that word on my screen, I was reminded of an experience that occurred some fifty years ago.

At the time, I was splayed face-down on a sweat-scented wrestling mat. Straddling me was Grant Wilke, a tough competitor whose strength and wrestling skills far surpassed my own. With my belly squashed against the mat and Grant's weight pressing firmly into my lower back, I attempted what high-school wrestlers call an "escape." Rising like a cobra and twisting backward, I inadvertently gave Grant a sharp elbow in the ribs.

"Oops!" said I.

"Don't say 'oops', Ben," Grant replied, casting a disdainful look in my direction. Not only had my clumsy move failed of its purpose. I had also offended Grant's sense of what a wrestler is supposed to be thinking, feeling, and saying. "Take that!" might have been more to the point. "Oops!" was not in the protocol.

Had I looked into my experience that afternoon, I might have divined that I was not cut out to be a wrestler. And had I looked into my offending word, I might also have made a few discoveries. "Oops" and its variant "Whoops" are words of unknown origin. They became current in American English in the 1920s. "Whoops" may allude to "whoop," as in "war whoop," and "Oops" may be its contraction. In any event, both words contain a long, low vowel, a plosive consonant ("p"), and a terminal sibilant ("s"), which together create a sound not unlike that of tire being punctured. Or one's pride, or poise, or public image.

To grammarians "Oops" is known as an interjection. Expressive, colorful, and often illogical in context, interjections reveal much about those who use them. If you say "Stone the crows!" when surprised, you are probably British and not as young as you used to be. Likewise "Holy mackerel, Andy!" which Kingfish frequently exclaimed on the *Amos 'n' Andy Show*, but only people of a certain age would say today. "Jeepers creepers!" my wife, Robin, likes to say, despite my telling her that no one says "Jeepers creepers" anymore. "Jeepers," she said last week, employing the shorter form.

Beyond the age and social background of the user, interjections also reveal the speaker's present state of mind. In the case of "oops," that state might be described as embarrassed, apologetic, and desirous of atonement. By contrast, "Uh-oh" connotes mild apprehension, "Yikes" astonishment, and "Ugh" disgust. Whatever the state being disclosed, however, interjections disclose it before we've had time to think about it, or modify it with thought, or disguise it with discursive language. At any given moment, our interjections may be no more than habitual verbal reflexes or escape valves for powerful feelings. But for those of us inclined to introspection, they can also provide clues to our ever-changing mental states and the causes that engender them. Rents, as it were, in the curtain of language, they can show us to ourselves.

In this respect, as in their spontaneous nature, interjections have a part to play in Zen practice. In his book *Zen Action, Zen Person*, the philosopher T.P. Kasulis describes Zen as a "prereflective" practice, by which he means a practice whose locus is the moment, prior to reflection, when a mental event occurs. That event might be a sensation, a passing thought, or an image from the past. Whatever it is, we experience it directly, without the mediation of conceptual thought. If we are diligent in the practice, we learn to experience ourselves and the world in this way, whether we are sitting on our cushions or going about our daily business. And interjections can help us, insofar as they constitute a direct, unmediated response to our experience. Knowing as much, Japanese Zen teachers have sometimes used interjections as wake-up calls, one of their favorites being the word *kwatz,* which has no extractable meaning. Uttered forcefully in a samurai's *basso profundo*, that bizarre word can restore the sleepiest practitioner to the here and now.

Of course it is often more pleasant to live in a dream of the past, a dream in which nothing has changed, and we are the same, unchanging selves that we were at the time. So it was one evening a few months back, when Robin and I sat on our couch, looking at my high-school yearbook. Arriving at the Sports section, we found black-and-white photos of my wrestling team. There, in his River Kings wrestling uniform, was Grant Wilke, who would go on to become a Marine Sergeant Major, a fire marshal, and a respected community leader. And there was I, an athletic-looking lad with conspicuous biceps, respectable pecs, and a calm, determined mien. No Adonis, to be sure, but a force to be reckoned with.

"You had a good build then," said Robin.

Oops.

2 June 2011

Contenders

"*I* coulda been a cont*en*der," laments the boxer Terry Malloy (Marlon Brando) in *On the Waterfront* (1954). "I coulda been *som*ebody instead of a bum . . ." If those lines are among the most famous in American film, it is perhaps because they express a familiar human desire. Which of us would not wish to be a "contender"? To be "somebody" in others' eyes?

Yet, as Shunryu Suzuki Roshi observes in his essay "Calmness of Mind," the desire to be "somebody" is costly to the human psyche. It steers us into trouble. And as Suzuki also observes, the desire to be somebody bears an intimate connection to the process of breathing, specifically inhalation. "When you are more interested in inhaling than in exhaling," he notes, "you easily become quite angry. You are always trying to be alive." When we are inhaling, we are "trying to be active and special and to accomplish something." And when, in meditation, we make our inhalations the main focus of our attention, we may only add to our anxiety. In Suzuki's view, conscious inhalation, striving, and the drive to be somebody are of a piece, and all conduce to suffering.

As an alternative, Suzuki advises us to concentrate on our exhalations:

> *First practice smoothly exhaling, then inhaling. Calmness of mind is beyond the end of your exhalation. If you exhale smoothly, without even trying to exhale, you are entering into the complete perfect calmness of your mind. You do not exist anymore. When you exhale this way, then naturally your inhalation will start from there. All that fresh blood bringing everything from outside will pervade your body. You are completely refreshed. Then you start to exhale, to extend that fresh feeling into emptiness.*

If we practice in this fashion, Suzuki goes on to say, we will "gradually fade into emptiness—empty, white paper." In so doing, we "can feel like being at our mother's bosom, and we will feel as though she will take care of us."

To those accustomed to feeling pride in their achievements and excitement in the act of striving, Suzuki's advice might seem wide of the mark. What's wrong with puffing out one's chest when one has completed a project with flying colors, or earned a promotion, or received a coveted award? What's wrong with being a contender? And conversely, why should anyone want to be an empty, white paper? In a culture of relentless self-promotion, Suzuki's admonition might seem a recipe for self-annihilation or self-inflicted failure. And even those of a more modest nature might justly resist a practice that fails to acknowledge our deep-seated need for personal recognition. Such a practice would at best be incomplete and at worst self-deceptive.

Fortunately, Suzuki Roshi was not among those Zen teachers who advocate, or appear to advocate, extinction of self as a condition of awakening. In the passage quoted above, Suzuki acknowledges that when we inhale, we bring "fresh blood" into our bodies. And elsewhere he notes that after a full exhalation, when we once again inhale, we "come back" to ourselves "with some color or form." What Suzuki is proposing is not the extinction of self but a redress of an imbalance—a reordering, as it were, of priorities. When we focus on the in-breath, we are supporting what Suzuki calls the "small self," the self whose first concern is its own survival. By contrast, when we focus on the out-breath, we are attending to the "big self": to interdependent reality, of which the small self is only a part. Focusing on our in-breath, we separate our small selves from the web of life; focusing on our out-breath, we "gradually vanish," reentering the stream of moment-to-moment living.

In Zen teachings, "small self" and "big self" correspond to the "relative" and "absolute" dimensions of our experience. And these, in turn, are represented by the analogy of a wave and water. In that analogy, the wave represents the relative dimension, where conditioned forms arise, endure for a time, and eventually dissolve. By contrast, water represents the formless, ultimate dimension, from which all forms arise and to which they return. Breathing in, we renew our sense of a personal self, our existence in the relative dimension. We become contenders, and more power to us. Breathing out, we recognize that in absolute reality, all conditioned forms, including the one we have just created, are subject to dissolution. They are on their way out. Practicing in this way, we maintain our balance, our realism, and our inner peace.

16 June 2011

An Appropriate Response

In 1968 the Vietnamese Zen master Thich Nhat Hanh, then a young Buddhist monk, visited the United States. Meeting with church groups, students, and others, he sought to promote peace and reconciliation. Throughout his tour, the gentle monk was well-received, but when he spoke one evening at a wealthy church in St. Louis, he found himself confronted by an angry detractor, who stood up to challenge him. "If you care so much about your people," demanded the man, "why are you here? If you care so much for the people who are wounded, why don't you spend your time with them?" Taken by surprise, Thich Nhat Hanh had no choice but to respond. But what could he say? What might be an appropriate response?

That question resounds throughout the Zen tradition. As the Zen priest Norman Fischer observes, Zen is less about "solitary visionary experience than the saving possibility of human relationship . . . . Enlightenment is the fruit not of isolation but of connection. Zen is the practice of compassionate and warmhearted relationship." And as the Chan master Yunmen Wenyan (864–949 CE) observed, eleven centuries earlier, Zen practice is chiefly concerned with cultivating an "appropriate response" to the circumstances of our lives. Unless we are hermits, those circumstances will include our fellow human beings, especially those in closest proximity. When conflict arises, how can Zen training help us to respond, compassionately and wisely? What are the components of an appropriate response?

To begin with, Zen teachings advise us to respond in ways appropriate to the occasion. When the American poet Elizabeth Bishop was asked a series of questions about the art of poetry, she replied that "it all depends. It all depends on the particular poem one happens to be trying to write." And from the vantage point of Zen teachings, the same holds true for the trying situations in our lives, whether the "other" be someone blasting rock music into our backyard, or a telemarketer interrupting our dinner, or a resident woodchuck eating the flowers in our garden. Our response may be brisk or deliberate, gentle or forceful, reasoned or instinctive. But whatever it is, it will honor the conditions peculiar to the immediate situation.

At the same time, that response will also be consistent with our deepest values. It will express our deepest, best intentions. In his essay "The Heart's Intention," the meditation teacher Phillip Moffitt explains the practice of "right intention," in which we seek to align our actions with our values, specifically the value known as *ahimsa*, or non-harming:

> *Imagine that you will have a difficult interaction later today. If you are not mindful of your intention, you might respond to the situation with a harmful physical action—*

maybe because you got caught in your fear, panic, greed, or ill will. But with awareness of your intention, you would refrain from responding physically. Instead, you might only say something unskillful, causing much less harm. Or, if you have a habit of speaking harshly, with right intention you might only have a negative thought but find the ability to refrain from uttering words you would later regret. When you're grounded in your intention, you are never helpless in how you react to any event in your life.

As Moffitt acknowledges, the practice of aligning our actions with our values is not primarily rational. "Life is so confusing," he notes, "and emotionally confounding that the rational mind is unable to provide an absolutely clear intention." Instead we must rely on our "intuitive knowing," our "felt wisdom," which we cultivate through the practice of meditation. By learning to reconnect with our best intentions while practicing meditation, we develop the ability to do the same when responding to difficult, everyday situations.

If we are practicing Zen meditation in particular, we may also learn to view our reactions and responses in a broader, less personal perspective. When we practice *zazen*, or seated meditation, we settle into an awareness of interdependent reality. Although we are sitting as still as we can manage, we are aware of fluctuating conditions, within and around us. Those conditions may include bodily tensions and external sounds, the flow of our breath or the roar of an accelerating car. Grounded in that awareness and guided by that perspective, we can learn to view our rising thoughts, feelings, and reactions, however pleasing or troubling, habitual or fresh, as no more important than the other phenomena we are encountering. And as we carry that awareness into everyday life, we can learn to respond to difficult situations with egoless compassion rather than react out of fear and anger.

So it was with Thich Nhat Hanh, who responded to his challenger in a way that reflected his rigorous monastic training. Although he was inwardly upset and wanted to react with anger, he practiced conscious breathing until he found a better way. "If you want the tree to grow," he said, "it won't help to water the leaves. You have to water the roots. Many of the roots of the war are here, in your country. To help the people who are to be bombed, to try to protect them from this suffering, I have to come here." By speaking those words, quietly and calmly, Thich Nhat Hanh pacified his adversary, and he transformed the tense atmosphere of the room. In the midst of potential harm, he offered an appropriate response.

30 June 2011

The Backward Step

"It's time for Congress to step up to its job," writes Chris Dunn on his blog *Collegiate Times*. "It's time for the Lakers to step up," writes Darius Soriano on the *Forum Blue and Gold*. "It is time for webOS to step up," writes Derek Kessler on *www.precentral.net*, if Hewlett-Packard is to compete with the iPad. And "it is time to step up and be found faithful to God and his work," writes Pastor Joe on the website of the Oakdale Baptist Church.

Surveying these pronouncements, one might conclude that it is time for American bloggers—and American popular culture—to find a new figure of speech. But cliches often reflect common beliefs, and behind this particular cliche lies a widely held belief that whatever the problem might be, it can best be addressed by someone stepping up. Whether the field of endeavor be politics, sports, business, or religion, this belief is so familiar as to be mistaken for empirical fact. And though the contexts in which it functions are most often practical, it also carries its share of moral weight. Those who have stepped up are to be commended. Those who have not would do well to get with the program.

"Stepping up" is shorthand for "stepping up to the plate." In its most common usage, the phrase means to assume responsibility, to become accountable. It may also refer to action in the service of a cause. As with baseball, so with our actions in the world: stepping up to the plate requires skill, courage, and initiative. In many situations, especially those involving political corruption, social injustice, or racial discrimination, stepping up to the plate is exactly what is called for. "He stands like a gaunt lighthouse of honesty," wrote Ernest Hemingway of his friend Herbert Mathews. And the same might be said of the leading activists of our time—Nelson Mandela, Martin Luther King, Aung San Suu Kyi, to name a few. Their work has left a mighty wake, as has their moral example.

Yet as the great contemplative traditions, Zen included, remind us, self-assertive action, however noble or necessary, is only one mode of being. Stepping forward is only one way of meeting the world. And in one classic text of the Soto Zen tradition, Eihei Dogen's *Fukanzazengi* (*Recommending Zen to All People*), the practitioner is admonished to do the very opposite:

> *Stop searching for phrases and chasing after words. Take the backward step and turn the light inward. Your body-mind of itself will drop away, and your original face will appear. If you want to attain just this, immediately practice just this.*

In this passage the phrase "just this" refers to undifferentiated reality: whatever is happening, within and around us, in this very moment. That reality cannot be grasped by concepts or described in words, which divide the totality into its constituent parts. But the wholeness of our experience can be realized by taking "the backward step," which is to say, by shifting one's orientation from ego-centered thinking to selfless awareness. In the light of that awareness, what is occurring in the mind and body becomes luminously clear.

Dogen's formulation is abstract, but it can be illustrated by a concrete example. Let us say that you are an avid gardener, and as you walk down the sidewalk on a midsummer evening, you are thinking about your gardens. Lately, you note, the deer have been roaming your backyard and devouring your red-twigged dogwoods. The woodchucks have also been busy, eating your phlox and destroying your bachelor buttons. And just yesterday you noticed that slugs have been attacking your marigolds. Perhaps you should put out slug bait. Or put out a shallow bowl of beer, which the slugs can imbibe until they drown. You can use almost any kind of beer, with the possible exception of Pabst, which even a slug might be smart enough to avoid . . . .

Such is your train of thought, which a car's loud horn brings to an end. Waking from your reverie, you realize that you are walking on a cracked, uneven sidewalk. Looking around, you also realize that you have walked the better part of a block without noticing a thing. Not the storm clouds gathering in the west, nor the chill in the air, nor your own thoughts as they have come and gone. As you settle into your newly awakened state, you notice that thoughts are still arriving, but now you are aware of their arrivals, as you are of your immediate surroundings. Although you are still moving forward, you have taken the backward step.

In urging us to take that step, Dogen is not suggesting that we remain forever in a state of pure being—or culpable inaction. Rather, he is urging us to inhabit our experience, naturally, spontaneously, and completely, in the very moment when it is occurring. Elsewhere in his teachings, Dogen speaks of a rhythm of backward and forward steps, by which he means a reciprocal relationship of thinking and awareness. Stepping forward, we think, speak, and act; stepping back, we cultivate awareness of what we are doing. In this way we learn to look deeply into our thoughts, words, and actions, even as we are stepping up.

15 July 2011

Inhabiting Zen

To live in a place is one thing, to inhabit it another. The word inhabit derives from the Latin *inhabitare*, which originally meant *to dwell*. "They shall build houses," prophesied Isaiah, "and inhabit them; and they shall plant vineyards, and eat the fruit of them" (*Isaiah* 65:21). To eat the fruit of your vineyards, you cannot be flitting from one locality to another. You must dwell in one place for a while.

What is true of grape farming is also true of the practice of Zen. "Authentic Zen," writes Dr. James H. Austin, a neurologist and longtime Zen practitioner, "has always meant inhabiting each present moment in the most natural, direct, and spontaneous way." And in his book *Being Upright*, the Zen priest Tenshin Reb Anderson employs the same verb to describe the practice of *zazen*:

> *For a sentient being to practice the ultimate good means not to move. How do you realize not moving? By fully settling into all aspects of your experience: your feelings and*

your perceptions. Not moving means to be fully congruent with yourself. You go down to the bottom of your experience, as all buddha ancestors have done, and enter the proverbial green dragon's cave. Graciously and gently, you encourage yourself to fully inhabit your body, speech, and thought. You may even command yourself to be obedient to yourself, and to come all the way in and sit down.

"Although no one issues the invitation," Anderson further explains, we "invite the self into the self." As both "host and guest of the self," we fully inhabit our experience.

That process can commence with recognition of our physical environment. Just as movies often open with a bird's-eye view of a city or a panoramic view of a landscape, we can begin a sitting by surveying the room in which we are practicing. How large or small is the space? How bright or dim the light? How cold or warm, dry or humid is the air? What are the ambient sounds, and how long does any new sound last? By asking such questions—or, more intuitively, by feeling our way into our environment—we reconcile ourselves with our surroundings, however pleasant or not-so-pleasant they might be.

Having attuned ourselves to the place in which we're sitting, we can turn our attention to our own presence within that place. We can fully inhabit our bodies. If we are at ease with our physical selves, we might have already settled into stillness. If not, it can be helpful to recite the *gatha*, "Breathing in, I am aware of my body / Breathing out, I release the tensions in my body," letting these phrases accompany our inhalations and exhalations. If we continue in this vein for five minutes or more, we may discover—or re-discover—that we are not solid objects set into a foreign or familiar space. Rather, we are breathing organisms in constant interaction with whatever is occurring, within and around us. If we are practicing with others, we may notice how the smells of cologne or perfume or even a freshly laundered shirt affect us, or how the slightest rustle of clothing resonates within us. If we are practicing alone, we may notice how external sounds—the hum of a fridge, the racket of a passing motorbike—create or release tensions in our bodies.

Noticing these things, we may also notice what the eighteenth-century master Menzan Zuiho Zenji called the "frozen blockage of emotion-thought": the worries and fears, cravings and aversions that we carry into meditation. Defining "emotion-thought" as a "stubborn attachment to a one-sided point of view formed by our own conditioned perception," Menzan urged us to bring effortless awareness to that attachment. By so doing, we clarify "how emotion-thought melts" in the light of mindful awareness. In the passage quoted above, Tenshin Reb Anderson offers similar instruction, enjoining us to settle into our feelings and perceptions and to "fully inhabit [our] body, speech, and thought." Rather than try to cut off thoughts and their emotional subtexts, we watch their comings and goings. Rather than repress our mental activities, we dwell in our awareness of their presence.

If we continue to sit in this way, we can indeed "go down to the bottom of [our] experience." We can inhabit the ground of being. By settling peacefully into our surroundings, our bodies, our feelings, and our perceptions, we can discern the causes and conditions that have created our present experience, and we can realize our place in the dynamic, interdependent web of life. In the words of Shohaku Okumura, we can "participate with the whole universe as it practices through our individual bodies and minds," and "allow the universal life force to practice *through* us for all beings." And paradoxically, by relinquishing the notion of a separate self—a self absorbed in its likes and dislikes, its comforts and discomforts—we can give our unique and individual selves their fullest expression.

When that occurs, we will not only become most fully ourselves. We will also continue the long line of Zen practitioners, which spans a period of more than fifteen hundred years. "When the Horse-master becomes the Horse-master," wrote Eihei Dogen Zenji, "Zen becomes Zen." By fully inhabiting ourselves, we also inhabit Zen.

11 August 2011

A Life's Work

*I*f you have ever sung in a choir, you know that certain disciplines apply. You must sit up straight at the edge of your chair. You must breathe from the diaphragm. And you must open your mouth more widely than you otherwise would—widely enough to accommodate three fingers. Although these principles are simple, it is easy to forget them, especially if your mind is elsewhere.

Such was the case one morning in 1961, when I and other members of the Clinton High School A Cappella Choir sat upright at the edge of our chairs, rehearsing Michael Pretorius's beautiful carol "Lo, How a Rose E'er Blooming." Leading us was our director, John De Haan, a tall, ruggedly-built man with a gentle but commanding presence. Glancing in my direction, he noticed my half-open mouth. "Open your mouth, Ben," he said, quietly but firmly, in his deep bass voice. "This is my life's work."

Although I was only sixteen at the time, I did not fail to recognize John De Haan's profound commitment to the art of music. I opened my mouth. In the decades since, I have observed that same deep sense of vocation in friends, colleagues, and acquaintances, whether their line of work has been college teaching or musical performance, artistic creation or law enforcement, dentistry or the ministry. And I have found it particularly conspicuous among Zen teachers and practitioners, who are engaged in what the Zen-trained teacher Toni Packer has called "the work of this moment." For one of the chief aims of Zen practice is to attain a continuous awareness of what is occurring, within and around us. That job is endless, and it requires total presence of mind. For the dedicated Zen practitioner, it might be said, one's very life becomes one's life's work.

In formal Rinzai Zen, multiple practices support that work. There is, to begin with, the central practice of *zazen*, or seated meditation, in which we begin by following the breath and proceed to a direct encounter with ourselves and our surroundings. There is the practice of chanting, which reunites body, breath, and mind and grounds us in the here and now. There is *samu*, or work practice, in which we commit full attention to the task at hand, and *kinhin*, or walking meditation, in which we walk for the sake of walking. There is the practice of bowing, which heightens our social awareness and promotes attitudes of gratitude and respect. And, not least, there is the practice of *dokusan*—the face-to-face interview between student and teacher, in which the student reports on his or her practice, and the teacher responds. All of these practices help us "come back to presence," as Zoketsu Norman Fischer ably puts it. They strengthen our ability to be present, both for ourselves and other people.

With respect to our relationships with others, the practice of dokusan deserves special mention. Also known as *san-*

zen, that practice commences when the teacher rings a hand bell, and the student, who has been sitting in zazen, responds by striking a larger bell. Moments later, the student arrives at the dokusan room, makes three bows and a prostration, and sits in the *seiza* (kneeling) position before the teacher. What follows will depend on present conditions, including the student's depth of insight, the role (if any) of Zen koans in the practice, and the respective states of mind of student and teacher. The teacher may question the student, or sharply correct erroneous perceptions, or merely listen. Pithy advice ("Just sit!") may be offered—or none at all. Yet in my experience one rarely leaves the dokusan room without feeling that something important if not momentous has just occurred. Two minds have met, in a way that minds rarely do.

To replicate the depth and intensity of dokusan in one's everyday encounters is not always appropriate or desirable. In polite conversation it is not the norm, and it can come across as unnaturally earnest, if not offensively assertive. But to develop the *capacity* for such exchange is both a formidable challenge and a worthy objective. Just as John De Haan devoted his life to creating complex polyphonic music, we can endeavor to treat each of our meetings in the spirit of *ichigo ichie*: as "one time, one meeting," unprecedented and unrepeatable. Through successive acts of single-minded attention, we can cultivate wisdom, compassion, and equanimity in a world of turmoil. Although such a practice is unlikely to make us rich, famous, or materially successful, it is work enough for one life.

25 August 2011

Being Positive

When Ernest Hemingway was a cub reporter for the *Kansas City Star*, he learned four simple rules for writing well:

1. Use short sentences.
2. Use short first paragraphs.
3. Use vigorous language.
4. Be positive, not negative.

"Those were the best rules I ever learned for the business of writing," Hemingway later declared. "I've never forgotten them. No man with any talent, who feels and writes truly about the thing he is trying to say, can fail to write well if he abides with them."

To anyone familiar with Hemingway's prose, the first three rules will come as no surprise. However, the fourth might give the reader pause, insofar as it connotes an intentionally optimistic outlook. Was the author of *A Farewell to Arms* promoting the power of positive thinking? Was Papa urging us to put on a happy face?

Probably not. What Hemingway was advising us to do, at least as writers, was rather more technical than that. He was admonishing the writer to pay attention to what is present, not what is absent, and to render the present reality in the most direct way. Don't say that a stomach cramp is less than pleasant. Say that it hurts.

Ernest Hemingway was not a Zen practitioner, but by and large, Zen teachings accord with his rules. Zen is famously a practice of few words—or none at all. And the heart of the practice is mindfulness, which Zen master Thich Nhat Hanh defines as being present for the present moment. Practicing seated meditation, we do not focus on what is missing in our immediate experience. We attend to what is present, be it a physical sensation, a transitory feeling, a passing thought, or a state of mind. And time and again we return to our breathing, which is unmistakably present and brings us back to the present moment. For some practitioners, the use of minimal language ("in/out," "deep/slow") serves to support the practice of conscious breathing.

Yet, as Hemingway well knew, the English language runs athwart the purpose of being positive, abounding as it does in negative nouns and verbs, prefixes and suffixes, adjectives and adverbs. Most words ending in "-less" (*homeless, speechless, clueless*) describe an absence, as do words beginning with "in" or "un" (*inarticulate, insubstantial, unwholesome, unprepossessing*). Beyond that, rhetorical devices such as *litotes*, a form of understatement that indicates what is not there ("I'm not partial to Brussels sprouts") and *antithesis* ("I had a wonderful evening," quipped Groucho Marx, "but this wasn't it"), call attention to what is missing. Most conspicuously, the subjunctive mood ("had we but world enough, and time"), tempts us at every turn to state what might have been, or might yet be, rather than what is.

As with human language, so with the human mind. "Is it just that humans are wired," asks Roshi John Sutherland, "to yearn for the thing that isn't there?" The answer is almost certainly yes, whether the object of attention be our selves or the world at large. Who among us hasn't looked in the mirror and noted a shortfall or two? And given the present state of the world economy, the unending violence in unstable foreign nations, and our own dysfunctional government here at home, who can be blamed for focusing on what is lacking rather than what is present? If we are indeed to be positive, both in Hemingway's sense and in the more conventional sense of being optimistic, how should we go about it? Where should we look for enabling models?

One place might be James Joyce's *Dubliners* (1914), a pivotal work in Hemingway's development and the primary model for his debut collection of stories, *In Our Time* (1925). In his pioneering work Joyce set out to portray the moral, emotional, and spiritual "paralysis" of Great Britain's second city. To that end he employed what he called a "scrupulous meanness" of style, void of verbal excess. Focusing, respectively, on childhood, adolescence, maturity, and public life, Joyce depicted repressed, lower-middle-class lives, straitened by economic hardship, constrained by a narrow nationalism, and oppressed by a culpable religious hierarchy. Yet if Joyce's style and content are largely negative, his stories' impact is quite the opposite. Their extraordinary concentration and economy of means have a bracing effect, leaving the reader feeling more exhilarated than depressed. Their realism is life-affirming.

Much the same might be said of Zen meditation, which also brings a concentrated mind to bear upon realities, some of them unpleasant. Sitting still for forty minutes or more, we become intimate with our memories, fears, fantasies, and expectations, our habitual judgments of ourselves and others. We may also meet what Carl Jung called our "shadow" self, the one we hide from the world. Such encounters can be disturbing, but if we are paying close attention, we may also notice that what we are encountering is, in the language of Zen, empty of a separate self. It arises, abides, and dissipates, like contrails in the sky. And if we sit for days on end, as happens in a meditative retreat, we may also discover that facing realities feels better than the alternative. It tests our moral strength, and it reminds us, concretely and irrefutably, that we are alive, in flux, and inextricably connected to other living beings. I know of no surer way of being positive.

8 September 2011

In the Waiting Room

*I*magine, if you will, that you have just arrived at your local hospital for a routine test. Anticipating a wait, you have brought a book. After checking in at the reception desk, you seat yourself in a plastic chair and open your book.

Very soon, however, you discover that you are unable to concentrate, because you are being bombarded by the sounds of daytime TV. Muzak you could handle, but not the dialogue of a soap opera, which is keeping you from reading the words on the page. You can't enjoy your book, but you can't leave either. For a while you contain your frustration, but when it becomes intolerable, you go to the reception desk to complain. There you learn that the hospital keeps the TV on because most patients want it on. A survey indicated as much. So you return to your seat, humbled and disgruntled.

Most of us, I suspect, have had an experience of that kind. Whether it be the aural abrasion of someone yakking on a cell phone, or, in today's airports, the drone of CNN transforming human pain into entertainment, the ambient racket in public spaces grows louder and more continuous by the day. Quiet spaces, even in formerly quiet places, are becoming ever more difficult to find. Apparently many people prefer—or are willing to tolerate–a cacophonous environment. But what, if anything, are the rest of us to do?

One obvious solution is to shut the distractions out. Earplugs can sometimes do the trick, as can the earphones of an iPod. If that doesn't work, it may be possible to stop the noise, or have it reduced, by complaining to the appropriate authority. Those measures failing, we can occupy ourselves with our BlackBerries or some other electronic device, if we have one. Or we can hunker down and wait it out, nursing our sense of separation, our fantasies of moral superiority, our low opinion of those who are disturbing our peace.

There is, however, another option, which on first hearing might sound counter-intuitive. That option, simply put, is to be present for the sounds we so abhor: to listen to the noise with openness and full attention, as one might listen to a string quartet by Mozart. For some that task might be a challenge, and a pointless one at that. But for those who can manage it, the exercise can illuminate the nature of suffering and foster some useful discoveries.

Three years ago, the writer and Zen teacher Roshi Joan Halifax slipped and fell on a bathroom floor, shattering her upper femur. Transported to Toronto Western Hospital, she learned that her injury would require immediate surgery. As it happened, however, her surgery was delayed, and for the next thirty hours Roshi Joan lay in the Emergency Room, tied to a gurney. Although she was in pain and had lost a great deal of blood, she engaged in a Tibetan

Buddhist practice known as *tonglen*, in which the practitioner breathes in the suffering of others and breathes out a healing calm. Aware, as she put it, of the "numberless beings who streamed through the doors on a busy Friday the thirteenth weekend," she practiced tonglen in their behalf. Rather than resist her surroundings, she opened herself to the suffering of those around her.

Roshi Joan Halifax has been practicing Zen meditation and working with the dying for more than forty years. Not all of us can follow her example. But with a little effort any one of us can anchor ourselves in conscious breathing and resolve to take in what the thirteenth-century Zen master Dogen called the totality of our experience. If we happen to be sitting in a hospital waiting room, that totality might include the presence of daytime TV. But it will almost certainly include the presence of anxiety—the anxiety of people who are there because their health or that of their loved ones is in question, if not in jeopardy. Daytime TV can be an anodyne, distracting the anxious mind by giving it something to do. Viewed in that way, its presence becomes understandable and even benign, if not uniformly desirable.

And should we turn our awareness inward, we might also examine our own habits of mind, particularly the propensity to extract, or attempt to extract, the good and the pleasant from the whole of our experience. As Alan Watts observes in *The Way of Zen*, one of the aims of Zen practice is to "see through the universal illusion that what is pleasant or good may be wrested from what is painful or evil." Opening ourselves, at once, to the bad and the good, the pleasant and the painful, we may at last divest ourselves of that illusion, while also cultivating a more compassionate heart. "Hospitals are houses of great suffering," observed Roshi Joan a few days after her surgery. "They are also places where acts of kindness and patience are boundless."

22 September 2011

The Music of What Happens

Now that the leaves are falling, and the hills are splashed with color, I'm reminded of an autumnal poem by the twelfth-century Japanese poet Saigyo:

> INSECTS ON AN EVENING ROAD
> On the road with not a soul
> to keep me company,
> as evening falls
> katydids lift their voices
> and cheer me along
>
> *Uchigusuru*
> *hito naki michi no*
> *yusare wa*
> *koe nite okuru*
> *kutsuwamushi kana*

In these lines the poet Saigyo, who was once a samurai and became a wandering monk, portrays himself as a solitary traveler. He takes comfort in the song of the *kutsuwamushi*, or giant cricket, which is known in Japan as the "bridle-bit insect" because its clacking sound resembles that of a bridle-bit in a horse's mouth. Heard from a distance, the song of the kutsuwamushi makes pleasant company.

Saigyo was not the first Japanese poet to relish the sound of singing insects. As the Irish writer Lafcadio Hearn observes in his essay "Insect-Musicians" (1898), night-singing insects occupy a place of honor in Japanese poetry, ancient and modern, where they are often associated with autumnal melancholy. "With its color-changes," writes Hearn, "its leaf-whirlings, and the ghostly plaint of its insect-voices, autumn Buddhistically symbolizes impermanency, the certainty of bereavement, the pain that clings to desire, and the sadness of isolation." Like his forebears in the Japanese poetic tradition, Saigyo finds solace in the song of the kutsuwamushi, which assuages his loneliness and draws him closer to the natural world.

Something similar occurs in "Song," a poem by the Irish Nobel laureate Seamus Heaney (b. 1939):

> *A rowan like a lipsticked girl.*
> *Between the by-road and the main road*
> *Alder trees at a wet and dripping distance*
> *Stand off among the rushes.*
>
> *There are the mud-flowers of dialect*
> *And the immortelles of perfect pitch*
> *And that moment when the bird sings very close*
> *To the music of what happens.*

In the first stanza of this poem, Heaney contemplates two trees with resonances in Irish legend. In Celtic mythology the European rowan, whose leaves and berries turn red in autumn, is known as the Traveler's Tree. It is said to offer protection to the traveler. It is also associated with druidic culture, being the wood of choice for magician's staves, divining rods, and magic wands. Encountering the rowan, Heaney also encounters the alder, from whose wood the ancient Celts made ritual pipes and whistles. In Irish folklore, the trunk of the alder is thought to conceal doors to the supernatural. In some Irish legends, the first man came from the alder, the first woman from the rowan.

As Heaney dwells in this place of origins, contemplating the intersection of human, natural, and supernatural worlds, his attention turns to language and music. In the phrase "the mud-flowers of dialect," he suggests an organic connection between human speech and the local terrain, the flowers of human dialect and the mud from which they've sprung. Likewise, in "the immortelles of perfect pitch," he evokes an intimate connection between the sounds of the natural world and human musicians with absolute pitch, who can reproduce those sounds without external prompts. And in his closing line, he recalls the legend of Finn Mac Cool, who challenged the warriors of the Fianna—accomplished poets, all—to name the finest music in the world. The music of the lark over Dingle Bay, suggested one. The laughter of a young woman, suggested another. The bellowing of a stag, suggested a third. No, replied Finn Mac Cool. The finest music is "the music of what happens." The function of the songbird—and perhaps of the poet—is to "sing very close" to the reality of that music. Or, as Heaney has said elsewhere, to "stay close to the energies of generation."

"Nature," writes the American essayist Edward Hoagland, "seems to me infused with joy. Even the glistering snow is evidence, though burdensome by March, and October's dying leaves, parched by an internal trigger before the first frosts, turn gratuitously orange, red, and yellow, as beautiful as any plumage." To close the gap between the mind and the energies of generation, the alienated self and the joyous natural world, is an aim of the contemplative writer and the Zen practitioner alike. And it is also a general human desire, especially in our time, when so many people live lives remote from the rhythms of the natural world. Not everyone can express that desire in exquisite verse. But any one of us can restore the unity of self and nature. We have only to step outside, collect our minds, and listen to the music of what happens.

6 October 2011

Dramatis Personae

"*M*an is least himself," wrote Oscar Wilde in *The Critic as Artist,* "when he talks in his own person. Give him a mask, and he will tell you the truth."

Wilde was speaking of Shakespeare, who, in Wilde's view, revealed more of himself in his plays than he did in his sonnets. Over the years I have often recalled Wilde's maxim, and I have had occasion to test it against my experience, both as a teacher of imaginative writing and as the author of poems, essays, and a verse novella. And by and large I have found Wilde's notion to be true, though perhaps not in the way he intended.

During my tenure as Professor of English at Alfred University, I taught an advanced writing course called Dramatis Personae. In this course each student created a character—a mask, if you like—and wrote from that character's' vantage point throughout the semester. The first assignment was a dramatic monologue; subsequent assignments included familiar letters, diary-entries, and first-person narratives. By mid-semester, if there were fifteen students in the room, there were also fifteen characters, and toward the end of the course the students artfully combined their characters in scenes and stories. The final assignment was a valediction, in which the students bid farewell to the characters they had inhabited for the past three months.

As might be expected, Dramatis Personae drew students interested in theater and psychology as well as imaginative writing. With few exceptions, they took to the work with gusto, crossing boundaries of gender, age, and ethnic background. Among their more memorable creations were a concert pianist who placed a marble bust of his mother on the piano during his concerts; a nineteenth-century American Indian maiden; a feisty, teen-aged boy from the inner city; a seasoned, outspoken journalist with reactionary social views; and a harried suburban woman modeled after the author's mother. Perhaps out of deference, no one ventured to create an English professor, though one did create a venerable tree and managed to write from that standpoint.

To a contemporary reader, Dramatis Personae might sound like an early version of Second Life. But in spirit and purpose the course differed fundamentally from that online phenomenon, insofar as the intent of Second Life is to project one's present self into an "avatar" and live a life more exciting than one's own. For if Dramatis Personae served, in part, as a training ground for potential poets, playwrights, and novelists, it also provided a setting in which to cultivate—and often to demonstrate—imaginative empathy. Rather than foster self-concern, the course encouraged self-forgetfulness. Rather than promote the making of fantasies, it sponsored a difficult realism—that of seeing others as persons in their own right, rather than as figures in one's private psychodramas.

Practice what you preach, my mother used to say. And in the spring of 1991, after teaching Dramatis Personae for nearly two decades, I discovered a way of obeying that proverbial imperative. At the time I was immersed in the study of Irish history in general and mid-twentieth-century Ireland in particular. And early one morning, I found myself dwelling in Ireland in the 1940s and writing in the voice of a middle-aged American lexicographer, down on his luck, who had come to Ireland to heal his wounded psyche:

> *I can't begin to say what brought me here,*
> *Unless it be the Irish predilection*
> *For whiskey and horses, both of which entail*
> *A certain loss and a less-than-certain gain.*

Thus began a blank-verse monologue of some nine hundred lines, later entitled "The Word from Dublin, 1944." Over the next two and a half years, this monologue would be followed by five more of similar length, in which my unnamed lexicographer meditates on Irish history, his "bungled" personal life, and his violent century, exploring such themes as loss, dispossession, and reconciliation. In time, this sequence of monologues would become my book *Midcentury*, which is at once a verse novella and a book-length meditation. Apart from its integrated themes, what holds that book together is its "mask"—a narrator whom the Irish poet Patrick Chapman, in his review of *Midcentury*, likened to an Irish storyteller and described as "a man of our own time, slightly at odds with the ways of the world but human and recognizably one of us." And yet that all-too-human storyteller never lived. From first to last, he was a *persona*, a fictive presence whose voice and vision gave coherence to otherwise disparate events.

Drama and meditation are sometimes viewed as opposites, the one centered in conflict and catharsis, the other in the cultivation of inner peace. But the practices of dramatic writing and Zen meditation share a common objective, namely the study of the nature of the self. And what both practices can reveal is the extent to which that fabled entity is a fabrication, be it a character in a novel or the personal "self" we construct and re-construct from day to day. Having fabricated a fictive self, we are in a position to see how the mind can fashion a seemingly solid character out of thin air. And by practicing Zen meditation, we can come to see how we make characters of ourselves, constructing illusory, separate "selves" from the stream of discrete experiences and the dynamic web of life. That may or may not have been the truth that Oscar Wilde had in mind, but it is one of the most important fruits of meditative practice.

20 October 2011

Contemplative Memory

In his essay "Reading Oneself," the writer and teacher Sven Birkerts describes the experience of encountering a long-forgotten page of his own prose. As Birkerts tells the story, he agreed to read the book manuscript of a student whom he had taught many years before. When his former student arrived at their meeting, she brought both her manuscript and Birkerts' written evaluation of her work, which she had saved from her days in his course. Typed on the Selectric II he was using at the time, Birkerts' prose seemed foreign to its author:

> And suddenly there's this feeling, I've had it before—more and more in recent years. I am reading something I've written and I not only don't recognize the sentences—they've gone from me—I also don't quite map to the mind that produced them. It's very much like catching your shopwindow reflection for a split second before you realize it's you. Almost always, the shock is negative. I look like that? With

> these sentences it's the opposite. My eyes catch sight of what my hand did. Reading, I actually admire the images, the figures of speech, the confidence of the rhythm. Not the rhythm I would write in now. But I feel it as distinct.

For Birkerts this encounter with his younger self was comparable to contemplating an old photograph. "The looking," he observes, "is mainly about taking in the differences."

Birkerts' anecdote vividly illustrates what many people feel in later life: the long trajectory of one's experience, the felt discontinuity between one's earlier self and its present manifestation. But Birkerts' story also illustrates a mental faculty that Henri Bergson, in his *Matter and Memory* (1896), defined as "contemplative memory." Contrasting this faculty with "motoric" memory, which a musician employs when playing a piece by heart, Bergson identified three distinguishing components of contemplative memory.

First, the process is spontaneous: memories arise unsummoned, often in the form of images. They are not the result of an act of will. Second, the remembered experience is clearly seen as having occurred at a time and a place in the past. It has a date, and it is unrepeatable. And last, what is most prominent in the remembered experience is the difference between then and now. Conditions were different then, and so were we, and in remembering the experience, we are not reliving it. Rather, we are viewing the past from the vantage point of the present. When we do so, and when the previous two elements are also present, we are exercising "contemplative" memory, which Bergson regarded as the purest form of memory.

As even a few minutes' reflection will verify, few of our memories are so pure. In Sven Birkerts' case, the presence of a tangible document—a datable, typewritten page—kept him, as it were, on the contemplative track. He had little choice but to view the object of memory as a thing of the past. But in everyday life, the process of remembering is likely to be far more capricious, selective, and faulty. If the remembered experience is emotionally charged, we are more likely to be engulfed by it than to contemplate it in a spirit of disinterested inquiry. If it is a painful memory, we may find ourselves engaging in what psychologists call "therapeutic forgetting." And if the memory has a moral dimension, we may enlist it in the service of self-vindication, or self-glorification, or self-abasement. We may make it a means to an end, serving the ego's insatiable needs.

In Zen, as in other meditative practices, we train ourselves to do otherwise. By sitting still and following our breath, we also follow the flux of our experience. Almost certainly that experience will include passing thoughts, many of them memories or fragments thereof. Some of those memories may be fond. Others may be wrenching. But whatever they happen to be, we train ourselves to acknowledge them without dwelling on them, or analyzing them, or allowing ourselves to be swept away. In the language of the classic texts, we open ourselves to the "ten thousands joys" and the "ten thousand sorrows." But even as we contemplate the past, we remain grounded in the present—in our upright, stable posture, our full awareness of breathing. In this way we cultivate an intimate but balanced relationship with what we remember. And over time, this way of relating to the past becomes a way of being, which we carry from the cushion into our everyday lives.

So it was with the poet and Zen practitioner Matsuo Basho (1644-1694), who visited Kyoto, the former capital and cultural center of Japan, in 1690. Mindful of the city's illustrious past, he wrote one of his most celebrated haiku:

Even in Kyoto,
how I long for old Kyoto
when the cuckoo sings

In this poignant haiku, Basho records a moment of awakening, prompted by the cuckoo's two-note call. Acutely aware of what is present, Basho is also aware of his longing for what is not. What is present is the Kyoto of 1690; what is absent is the storied, glorious city of earlier centuries. Bringing contemplative awareness to bear upon his present state of mind, Basho acknowledges the arising of a universal human feeling. Bringing contemplative memory to bear upon an image from the past, he evokes the transitory nature of all conditioned things.

3 November 2011

The Virtues of Solitude

"*There* is this cave / In the air behind my body / That nobody is going to touch: / A cloister, a silence / Closing around a blossom of fire." So wrote the American poet James Wright (1927-1980) in his poem "The Jewel." Wright's images are enigmatic, in the way dreams are, but their import is clear. They evoke a place in the self that is silent, luminous, and inviolate.

"The Jewel" appeared in Wright's third collection of poems, *The Branch Will Not Break,* in 1963. Fifty years on, it is an open question whether the space envisioned by Wright is still to be found—or whether it is much valued in contemporary culture. On one side, there are the incursions of the State, the illicit wiretappings of the Bush years being the most obvious example. On another, there are the watchful eyes of the multinational corporations, whose databases abound with information once considered private. No less disturbing, at least to some of us, is the widespread, voluntary relinquishment of personal privacy to social media. As the psychologist and media analyst Sherry Turkle has observed, the Internet has proposed itself as the "architect of our intimacies." And for many people, especially the young people Turkle has interviewed in her research, the disclosure of once-private feelings by means of Facebook or Twitter has become integral to the establishment of those feelings. It is not enough to feel at loose ends on a Saturday morning. You must publish that feeling to the wide world and await a virtual response.

As both an astute social observer and the mother of a daughter who spends much of her life online, Sherry Turkle views the erosion of personal privacy with concern. Citing Mark Zuckerberg's pronouncement that privacy is "part of the discourse of the past," she urges a return to older norms of privacy, such as she knew in her youth, and a relearning of the "virtues of solitude." Unless I miss my guess, the first of those objectives is already out of reach. It would require a societal shift of attitude, a turning back of the modern tide. But where the reclaiming of solitude is concerned, change is not only possible but readily at hand. And toward that end, the great contemplative traditions, Zen included, have much to offer, both in general outlook and in concrete daily practices.

To begin with, the posture of meditation provides both sustenance and a sense of personal sovereignty. Sitting in an upright, relaxed position, cross-legged or on a chair, we nourish and renew our minds and bodies. We open the channels of breath and energy. And by adopting this posture, not only on the cushion but periodically throughout the day, we also restore our stability, physical and emotional. Zen master Thich Nhat Hanh recommends that as we sit, we recite the verses, "Aware of my stability, I breathe in / Enjoying the stability, I breathe out." By so doing, we become "masters of [our] minds and bodies" and "are not pulled hither and thither by the different actions of body, speech, and mind, in which [we] might otherwise drown." Well established in mindful awareness, we can freely choose whether to speak or act or go online—or divulge private information about our lives.

Beyond the restoration of stability, meditative practice also opens a private interior space, where thoughts and feelings can arrive, abide, and run their course, unhindered by judgment or repression. As Elizabeth Mattis-Namgyel, a practitioner of Tibetan Buddhism, puts it, meditative space "doesn't do—it allows." It "allows objects to come into being, to function, to expand, to contract, to move around, and to disappear without interference." For those unaccustomed to prolonged sitting, one of those "objects" might be the impulse to do something—anything—beside sit still: to "tweet" or "text" a friend, or otherwise reconnect with the outer world. Within the openness of meditative space, however, that impulse can be allowed to announce itself, make its case, and gradually dissipate, precipitating no immediate action. Later on, having gained some insight into our mental activities, we can indeed reconnect with other people, perhaps at a deeper level than we would have, had we merely obeyed a passing impulse or indulged a habit of connectivity.

And should we continue to reclaim the "virtues of solitude" through meditative practice, we may also find ourselves connecting vertically as well as horizontally, which is to say, connecting to what the Zen tradition calls *sunyata*, or absolute reality. Shinge Roko Sherry Chayat Roshi has likened that experience to sinking a taproot deeply into the soil, even as we sit. By giving full attention to the flux of our experience, we eventually reconnect with the ground of being, the realm of non-duality. Having deeply experienced that connection, we may wish more than ever to reconnect with others, but we will bring to our encounters more than our ego's usual striving. We will bring the wisdom of liberation, or what one school of Zen calls silent illumination.

Something of that kind occurs to the speaker of "The Jewel" in the closing lines of James Wright's poem. "When I stand upright in the wind," he reports, "My bones turn to dark emeralds." Whatever that image might mean to the individual reader, it embodies the insight of a man who knows the virtues of solitude and has kept the jewel of his private life intact. Having inhabited the cave that nobody is going to touch, he has made that experience present to the reader.

17 November 2011

The Elbow Does Not Bend Outward

"The elbow," Zen teachings tell us, "does not bend outward." As a longtime Zen practitioner, I have heard that saying more than once, but in recent years it has come to seem ever more germane.

That might have something to do with my growing older. On certain mornings, the elbow is not the only bodily component that doesn't want to bend outward—or inward, for that matter. But a reminder that elbows do not bend outward can be of benefit to all of us, regardless of age, not least because it returns our hyperactive minds to a physical reality. Beyond that, the saying might also provide a countervailing motto for the twenty-first century, particularly as it pertains to the tempo of our activities, the volume of our consumption, and the realism of our view of life.

If you are a musician or lover of music, you know how important tempo is to musical performance. Every musical composition, it might be said, has its optimal tempo. In classical music, such terms as *lento* and *adagio* indicate a range of possible tempi, but the range is not all that wide, and even within it, one tempo is likely to feel more suitable than another. Played too slowly—or, more likely, too fast—the piece being performed will not be fully realized and may well be sorely compromised.

What is true of musical performance is also true of the most mundane activity, be it raking leaves or attending to e-mail or unscrewing the lid of a jar. Each has its appropriate tempo; each can be nearly effortless if performed at that tempo. But to the extent that we devalue common chores or do them by rote, we may give scant attention to the pace at which we're working. Ignoring the inherent tempo of the task at hand, we may be unwittingly bending the elbow outward.

And as with the pace of our daily activities, so with the volume of our daily consumption. On many late-model cars, we can now monitor the correspondence between our car's speed and our consumption of energy. As the one goes up, so does the other. But there is no such gauge to monitor our personal consumption, and if you have ever practiced "mindful eating," as Zen master Thich Nhat Hanh advises us to do, you may have noticed how great the volume of food on a supersized plate can come to seem, once you have begun to eat slowly, silently, and with full attention. And the same might be said of the volume of acquisitions in our closets, storerooms, and basements, once we stop to examine it.

In this time of austerity, Americans been consuming less and saving more. We have become more mindful of our economy's fragility and our own economic limitations. But even as we've scaled down our consumption of material goods, many of us have ramped up our consumption of information. In his book *The Information Diet* (O'Reilly

Media, 2011), Clay Johnson notes the consequences of trying to bend that particular elbow outward: cognitive problems, lost time, lower productivity, forgetfulness, and the consumption of false information. As a counter-measure, he advocates an "information diet," in which we keep track of the amount and kinds of information we are ingesting. "A healthy information diet," he suggests, "means measuring your intake in hours, and placing some limits for yourself, and making the most out of your information-consuming time." For himself he prescribes a "cap of six hours a day of total, proactive information consumption."

Insofar as Clay Johnson is advocating mindfulness of conditions and limitations, his attitude parallels that of Zen practice, which also endeavors to reconnect us with our actual lives. And nowhere is that aim more evident than in the line of inquiry that Zen calls the Great Matter of life and death, where opportunities for self-deception abound. All of us know we will die, but few of us can bear to face that fact. Sarah Creed, a hospice nurse, reports that ninety-nine per cent of hospice patients understand that they're dying, but "one hundred per cent hope they're not." Yet even here, as in our everyday activities and our habits of consumption, realism is possible, and the image of the unbending elbow, taken as an object of contemplation, can be a valuable emblem. In his eulogy for the poet and Zen priest Zenshin Philip Whalen (1923-2002), the Reverend Myo Lahey reported that Whalen, who joked that he had "flunked hospice twice," coped with his condition by noting, "hour after hour, that the elbow does not bend outward." By so doing, he embraced the reality of his waning life.

That may sound like a bleak vocation, but for those who can manage it, the practice of honestly facing limitations can bring relief, energy, insight, and even joy. Such was the case for the Zen scholar D.T. Suzuki, who experienced a profound realization when suddenly the meaning of "the elbow does not bend outward" became clear to him. Formerly he had thought the phrase expressed "a kind of necessity," but of a sudden he saw that "this restriction was really freedom," the "true freedom" of aligning oneself with natural limitations. By respecting such restrictions we can learn to live, as Philip Whalen did, with dignity and freedom in a world where things are as they are, and elbows do not bend outward.

1 December 2011

Fresh Listening

"Can there be fresh speaking and fresh listening right now," asks the Zen-trained teacher Toni Packer, "undisturbed by what is known?"

Packer's question would be pertinent in any season, but it is especially so in the present season, when the usual holiday tunes are in the air, and what we are hearing is so well-known as to seem banal. Like it or not, here comes The Little Drummer Boy again—he and his drum. Given the familiarity of the old songs, is "fresh listening" possible? And if so, how shall we go about it?

As a general rule, Zen teachings would urge us to set aside our social conditioning and merely *listen*. So what if we've heard "Let it Snow" or "Hark, the Herald Angels Sing" a thousand times before? Can we not put our preferences in abeyance and listen with "beginner's mind"? Can we not become a child again?

Perhaps we can, but in my experience such efforts are only intermittently successful. Layers of conditioning block the way. As an alternative, I would suggest in this instance the way of the Western scholar rather than that of the Eastern meditative practitioner. Rather than try to wipe the slate clean, we might make the oft-heard song an object of historical study and disinterested contemplation.

Many possibilities suggest themselves, but one in particular stands out. If you are a parent, you may know the "traditional" carol "Good King Wenceslas" all too well. It is often the first tune assigned to children who are learning to play an instrument. What is the carol's provenance, we might inquire, and what is its cultural history? Of what does it consist, musically and thematically?

Published in 1853, "Good King Wenceslas" is at once a Victorian Christmas carol and a retelling of a medieval Czech legend. The carol recounts a good deed done by Wenceslas I (907-935), who was not in fact a king but a duke of Bohemia, noted for giving alms to widows, orphans, prisoners, and the poor. In 935 Wenceslas was assassinated on orders from his brother. Shortly thereafter, he was declared a saint and martyr, and the Holy Roman Emperor Otto I conferred on him the "regal dignity and title." Today King Wenceslas is the patron saint of the Czech Republic.

In the manner of a ballad, "Good King Wenceslas" depicts the king regaling himself on the feast of St. Stephen's Day (December 26). Turning aside from the festivities, he observes a peasant gathering fuel in the bitter cold. This sight prompts the king to summon a page and to depart with meat, wine, and pine logs to the peasant's forest home. Along the way, the page complains of the cold, and the king instructs him to follow in his regal footsteps through the snow. Warmed by the sainted king's steps, the page completes the journey, and the compassionate errand is accomplished.

The lyrics of "Good King Wenceslas" were written by John Mason Neale (1816-1866), clergyman, hymnist, and warden of an English alms-house. An amalgam of narrative, dramatic, and didactic elements, Neale's text features a brief dialogue between the querulous page and the generous king, and it ends with a simple homily, in which Christian men are exhorted to share their wealth and thereby "find blessing" for themselves.

Given its content, "Good King Wenceslas" might have been set to a solemn tune. As it happened, however, Neale and his collaborator, Thomas Helmore, chose a thirteenth-century spring carol entitled "Tempest adest floridum" ("It is time for flowering"). In its original version, this lively Swedish carol portrayed lusty clerics disporting with local virgins. A later version, modified for churches and schools, portrayed the clerics praising the Lord with pious conviction.

In keeping with its mixed origins, the spirit of "Good King Wenceslas" is both energetic and restrained, dancelike and ceremonial. The carol's energy derives chiefly from its underlying rhythm, which consists of units of two syllables, the stress falling on the first. Known to prosodists as trochaic, this aggressive rhythm can be heard in the opening line:

GOOD King / WEN-ces- / LAS looked / OUT

At the same time, all of the verses end on stressed syllables, with two such syllables in every other line:

WHEN the / SNOW lay / ROUND a- / BOUT
DEEP and / CRISP and / E- / VEN

Sung as half-notes, the terminal syllables impart a stately feeling. Together with the trochaic rhythm, this recurrent pattern creates a pleasing tension between exuberant celebration and regal restraint.

To be sure, not everyone has found the union of moral fable and virile carol a happy one. The composer Elizabeth Poston, editor of *The Penguin Book of Christmas Carols*, dismisses "Good King Wenceslas" as "the product of an unnatural marriage between Victorian whimsy and the thirteenth-century dance carol." The dance measure of the original, she contends, "sounds ridiculous to pseudo-religious words."

Ms. Poston may be right, but popular opinion has ruled otherwise. And in the end, the verdict must be left not to the mind of the specialist but to the ear of the listener. If you would like to listen afresh to "Good King Wenceslas," while also contemplating the moral beauty of compassionate action, I would recommend an exceptional rendition by the Westminster Cathedral Choir. This performance features Aled Jones (then a boy soprano) as the page and the extraordinary baritone Benjamin Luxon as the large-hearted king.

15 December 2011

The Practice of Peace

"Peace," writes Zen master Thich Nhat Hanh, "is made of peace. Peace is a living substance we build our lives with. It is not only made of discussions and treaties. To infuse our world with peace, we must walk in peace, speak with peace, and listen with peace."

As so described, peace is more than a noble goal. It is a practice for everyday life. Peace is to be cultivated not only by imagining a peaceful world, as John Lennon did, but also by walking, speaking, and listening in ways that embody a peaceful spirit. In Thich Nhat Hanh's school of Vietnamese Zen, these practices are known as "walking meditation," "loving speech," and "deep listening." Diligently pursued, these practices can, in Thich Nhat Hanh's words, "help heal the wounds that divide our nation and the world."

Walking meditation is common to most forms of Buddhist meditation. It can be done in a variety of ways, ranging from slow to fast, formal to informal. Known in Japanese Zen as *kinhin*, walking meditation serves in part to provide relief between long periods of sitting. In principle, at least, kinhin also provides a bridge between the stillness of *zazen* (sitting meditation) and the activities of everyday life. By practicing kinhin, we bring the concentration and awareness engendered by zazen into our bodily movements. Later, we can bring those same qualities into all aspects of our daily lives.

Walking meditation, as taught by Thich Nhat Hanh, incorporates the traditional aims of kinhin but adds another dimension, namely that of cultivating a peaceful body and mind. As Thich Nhat Hanh often points out, when we are anxious or filled with anger, we print the earth with anxious or angry steps. By practicing walking meditation, we can be kinder to the earth, and we can also cultivate peace within ourselves. "To lessen the unpleasant feeling brought about by anger," he observes, "we give our whole heart and mind to the practice of walking meditation, combining our breath with our steps and giving full attention to the contact between the soles of our feet and the earth." By so doing, we reclaim our calm, allowing us to look directly at our anger and ascertain its cause.

In similar fashion, the practice of "loving speech" enables the practitioner to use words in ways that do no harm and may actively promote a peaceful resolution of conflict. Thich Nhat Hanh quotes the Vietnamese proverb, "It doesn't cost anything to have loving speech." What it does require, especially when people are in conflict, is a clear and balanced mind. Those in conflict are advised to practice conscious breathing and refrain from speaking until their equanimity has been restored. Only then are they in a position to practice "loving speech."

For Thich Nhat Hanh, that practice consists of saying "only loving things." This guideline is easily misconstrued, especially by newcomers, as merely repressing anger or making nice. But as defined in the stern teachings of Thich Nhat Hanh, to practice loving speech is "to say the truth in a loving way, with nonviolence." It is to "tell the deepest kind of truth," using "the kind of speech the other person can understand and accept." Far from being an exercise in avoidance or self-repression, loving speech is a difficult practice, demanding not only a steady mind but also honesty, care, and tact on the part of the speaker. Simply put, we must think before we speak, and we must engage the compassionate heart as well as the analytic mind.

Loving speech is, of course, only one side of peaceful communication, the other being "deep listening." This practice, suggests Thich Nhat Hanh, has "one purpose: to help the other person suffer less." To that end, the practitioner is enjoined to give wholehearted attention to the other person's words, bringing non-judgmental awareness to whatever is being said, however accurate or inaccurate, true or false it may be. That isn't easy, and to some it may prove untenable. To support the practice, Thich Nhat Hanh recommends the verses, "Breathing in, I know that I am listening in order to make this person suffer less. / Breathing out, I remember the person in front of me suffers very much." Should that measure fail, he advises the practitioner to postpone the conversation, lest harm ensue. "We have to renew ourselves," he warns, "before continuing. It is important to know our limit."

In a world scarred by violence and rent by deep political divisions, the integrated practices of walking meditation, loving speech, and deep listening may appear naive, utopian, and far removed from the corridors of power. But such was not the case in September, 2003, when Thich Nhat Hanh came to Capitol Hill to speak at the Library of Congress and offer a three-day retreat. Nine members of Congress, eleven family members, and nine clergy attended the retreat, which focused on loving speech, deep listening, and the resolution of conflict. However idealistic Thich Nhat Hanh's effort may appear, its limited success kindles a spark of hope. Even in Washington, it confirmed, entrenched opponents can learn the practice of peace.

29 December 2011

Seventy Percent

If you have ever played a competitive sport, you have probably been exhorted to give 100 percent. Or, as the sports cliché would have it, "110 percent." And the attitude embodied in that exhortation extends well beyond the arena of athletics. Whether the field of activity be business or law, selling cars or playing tennis, giving 100 percent of one's effort and energy is widely regarded as a virtue, if not a moral imperative.

In the present American workplace, those fortunate enough to be employed might have little choice but to give 110—or 150—percent, day in and day out, to their jobs and sponsoring institutions. But for the conduct of everyday life, a wiser guideline may be found in the ancient Chinese practice of Tai Chi. At once a martial art and a contemplative discipline, Tai Chi is rooted in the Taoist tradition. And a cardinal principle of Tai Chi states that the practitioner should not exceed 70 percent of his or her physical capacity. As Bruce Frantzis, a contemporary Tai Chi master, explains, "[s]triving for 100 percent inherently produces tension and stress because as soon as you strain or go beyond your capacity, your body has a natural tendency to experience fear and to begin, even without you[r] being aware of it, to tense or shut down in response." By staying within the limit of 70 percent, you "can use your full effort and energy, but not to the point of strain."

In Tai Chi, the "70-percent rule" applies to every dimension of the practice, including the force behind your movements, the extension of your turns, twists, and stretches, and the length of your practice session. For example, in the move Carrying Tiger to Mountain, the practitioner repeatedly bends down on the right knee while advancing forward and moving the arms and hands in a spiraling motion. At the beginning, if you are capable of bending all the way to the floor, you bend no further than 70 percent. By so doing, you can give your full attention to developing the move, unhindered by fear or resistance. Later on, as your strength and flexibility increase, you can bend all the way. Likewise, if you are capable of doing forty minutes of vigorous Tai Chi, you practice for thirty, lengthening your sessions as your stamina increases.

As a longtime practitioner of Guang Ping Yang Tai Chi, I can attest to the efficacy of the "70-percent rule," not only in the practice of Tai Chi but also in daily life. With respect to Tai Chi practice, observance of the rule has enabled me to relax, pay closer attention to detail, and execute the form with greater fluidity. Beyond that, the rule has helped me to perform, without strain, such routine domestic chores as scraping an ice-glazed windshield or lifting a forty-pound bag or hauling a loaded trashcan to the curb. And, not least, I have found the rule applicable to mental as well as physical effort, particularly the practice of Zen.

When many of us detect a problem, we want to fix it. And for some of us that means fastening on the problem and examining it from all sides, as a dog might worry a bone. By remaining mindful of the 70-percent rule, we can learn to step back from obsessive problem-solving, allowing conditions and causes to reveal themselves and solutions to arise of their own accord. By releasing ourselves from *doing*, we can leave more time for *being*, which is to say, for steady contemplation or patient inquiry rather than grasping for immediate solutions. And we can open a space in which intuitive perception, in tandem with rational analysis, plays a role in the process of understanding.

In similar fashion, if we practice Zen meditation, the 70-percent rule can protect us from excessive concentration on any one component of the practice—breath, posture, the particulars of form—or, in a more general way, on meditation itself. When newcomers first experience the benefits of sitting, they sometimes behave like recent converts, believing that meditation can "do it all." If their practice happens to be Zen, they may sit for fifty minutes at a time and up to twelve hours in a day. For some, such striving is a requisite for full awakening, and if the practitioner is young and healthy enough, he or she may be able to sustain it for a time. But for older practitioners, an uncritical embracing of the harsher aspects of Zen training can be destructive of health and well-being. "Just as we should not idealize Zen masters," writes the Zen teacher Grace Schireson, "we should not idealize monastic training as a perfect lifestyle for all ages. Medical research suggests that getting enough sleep and a diet appropriate to one's personal needs is important for sustaining health." In essence a principle of moderation, the 70-percent rule can remind us to temper our enthusiasm with critical thought and our commitment to the practice with realistic expectations.

Tai Chi is not a science, and its foundational rule is not a rigid absolute. It is a flexible guideline, which like the practice of Zen must be adjusted to suit one's age, health, and relative fitness. But as Bruce Frantzis observes, the 70-percent rule, intelligently applied, can prevent people from "becoming heroes at the expense of their bodies." Please bear it in mind on these winter mornings, especially when shoveling snow.

9 February 2012

Paying Heed

One April morning, twenty-five years ago, I found myself speaking with an elderly Irish farmer in his newly ploughed field. At the time I was living in County Monaghan, a rural midland county on the border with Northern Ireland. Prior to coming to Ireland, I had been reading the poems of Patrick Kavanagh (1904-1967), who grew up on a farm in Monaghan and felt confined by the "black hills" of his native landscape. At the age of thirty-four Kavanagh left the family farm for Dublin and went on to become the most influential Irish poet of his time. The Irish Nobel laureate Seamus Heaney has acknowledged his debt to Kavanagh's work.

"I knew Paddy," the farmer told me, leaning on his spade. "His father was a shoemaker. His mother couldn't read or write. His fields were up there, over that hill. Paddy kept his books in his fence—in between the stones. I'd see him reading there for hours at a time. He was not a good farmer, not good at all. He paid no heed to his fields." As if to clinch the point, he drove his spade forcefully into the soil.

He paid no heed to his fields. What struck me about that comment was not so much its content as the farmer's choice of words, particularly the word *heed*, which seemed to have come from an earlier century. The 1971 edition of the *Oxford English Dictionary* defines *heed* as "careful attention, care, observation, regard" and notes that its usage is "now chiefly literary." Forty years on, at least in North America, it is rare to find the word on the page, much less in conversation. *Heed* has gone the way of the corset, the rotary dial phone, and my father's Royal Empress typewriter.

In formal, literary usage the noun *heed* is most often the object of the verb *take*. "Take heed, my dear," wrote the poet Matthew Prior in 1689, "time flies apace." More rarely, *heed* serves as the object of the verb *pay*, which has a rather different connotation. To *take heed* is to take note of, to grasp the significance of a thing or event or situation. But to *pay heed* is to extend oneself: to offer care and respect to the object of attention. Like its distant cousin "paying homage," paying heed may be an act of duty, but it can also be an act of generosity, requiring an expense of effort in the service of something or someone other than oneself.

Defined in that way, the act of paying heed has much in common with the practice of Zen. "Attention, attention, attention," wrote the poet and Zen master Ikkyu (1394-1481), when asked to define the essence of the practice. To follow the way of Zen is to pay sustained attention to whatever is occurring, within us and around us, in the present moment. Beyond that, it is to bring a particular *quality* of attention to things as they are: an intimate, inquisitive attention to whatever we encounter. Ideally, that attention is both wholehearted and continuous. From moment to moment, we pay heed to the world and to our lives.

Yet, as the Zen teacher Jan Chozen Bays reminds us, few of us live up to that ideal. Preoccupied with the past, the future, and our abstract thoughts, we habitually ignore the present moment. In her book *How to Train a Wild Elephant*, Bays proposes a counter-measure, which can serve to awaken us from our reveries. Periodically throughout the day, she suggests, we can ask ourselves the question, "What am I ignoring?" By so doing, we can attenuate our inner monologue and open our awareness to our surroundings:

> *Ignoring the countless sights, sensations, and sounds that impinge on our eyes, skin, and ears may be essential when we need to focus on getting tasks done, such as reading a book before an exam, writing a sensitive e-mail, or getting a high score on a video game, but all that sensory blocking takes energy. When we are able to let go of those invisible shields and open our awareness to all that surrounds us, it is like stepping out of a cramped, musty room and finding ourselves in a large alpine meadow.*

An antidote to excessive cogitation, this exercise is also a way of cultivating appreciation for our lives. Ceasing to ignore our sensory field, we avail ourselves of its spaciousness and beauty.

There is often wisdom in archaic phrases. Like the sayings of the elders, such phrases preserve vanishing perspectives: ways of seeing that have left or are leaving the world. It is fair to say that in a world of ubiquitous mobile devices and obsessive connectivity, the act of *paying heed*, like the phrase used to describe it, is itself endangered, if not already going extinct. In a culture enamored of its entertainments, Zen practice can help us return to our actual lives. In a world rife with distractions, it can help us pay heed to our fields.

23 February 2012

The Ego Filter

Let us imagine that it's a Friday afternoon, and you are driving on the New York State Thruway. You are in the passing lane, going seventy-five miles per hour. The car on your right is not slowing down, and the SUV behind you is fast approaching. You can see its emblazoned grill in your rearview mirror. You do not want to increase your speed, but the driver behind you is leaving you no choice.

As the SUV draws closer, you feel your heart rate increasing, your anger arising. You can't see the driver in your mirror, but you can well imagine him: an aggressive, insensitive lout, with no concern for anyone but himself. As you reluctantly speed up and move over, an epithet comes to mind, and you let it slip from your lips. It is not a nice word, but it gives you satisfaction.

Moments later, the SUV passes on your left, and you see that the driver is not a lout at all but a petite, professional-looking woman in her thirties, who is keeping her eyes on the road, apparently unaware of your distress. And a few minutes later, after she and her SUV have long since disappeared, you realize that your anger, too, has disappeared and your clarity of mind is slowly returning. It is as if a veil, through which you were viewing the world, has gradually been lifted.

Shodo Harada Roshi, a contemporary Rinzai Zen master, has coined a suggestive name for that veil. He calls it the "ego filter." In his book *Moon by the Window*, he describes its effect on the ways in which we experience the world:

> *When we look out the window at the moon, it is always the same moon. But if any thoughts or desires come between us and the moon, what we see changes completely. . . . When we live with no separation between ourselves and what we are experiencing, we know the truly bright and clear Mind that is our Original Nature. But as long as we carry around an ego filter, it's impossible to experience this.*

As can be inferred from these observations, the "ego filter" consists of thoughts and their emotional subtexts, which come between our minds and our immediate experience. The moon itself is constant, but the ego filter colors what we see.

Lest Shodo Harada's statement be misunderstood, it is important to note that the "ego" to which he refers is not that of Freudian theory. Nor is it quite the same as the "ego" of popular culture. In Freudian theory, the ego is one of three components of the psyche, the other two being the "id" and the "superego." The ego mediates between the instinctual energies of the id and the moral and social values embodied in the superego. These days Freud's theory is out of fashion, but his neutral, analytic term has survived in popular culture, where its aura is decidedly negative. In today's American vernacular, the word ego evokes the Big Me, the Number One whom the egocentric person is always looking out for.

As used in Zen teachings, *ego* has a rather different meaning. In his article "The Psychology of Zen Buddhism," the cross-cultural psychologist Reginald Pawle explains that in Zen the ego is seen not as the id's executor but as the "root of mind," the "principal operator" of the psyche. Zen teachings call it "discriminating mind," and its function is to make dualistic distinctions: up from down, left from right, pleasant from unpleasant, good from bad, and especially, "self" from "other." The ego picks and chooses, in accordance with our desires and aversions. Without it, we could not choose a detergent or read a map or wisely invest our savings. Indeed, we could not safely cross a busy street, much less drive a car.

Yet in Zen teachings the ego is also seen as the primary source of suffering, insofar as we identify with our preferences or posit a solid, separate, choice-making self. It is one thing to choose miso soup over cheeseburgers, PBS over Fox News, a Prius over a Hummer. It is another to conjure an immutable self who makes such choices, irrespective of changing conditions. "If you're not sure whether you own an iron," reads an ad for a popular men's deodorant, "you're a Mitchum man." By such formulations, we reify our attitudes, beliefs, and patterns of behavior into fictive selves. More harmfully, we separate our illusory selves from others, and we pit our race, religion, gender, or economic class against the rest of humanity. By nurturing such habits of thought, Zen teachings tell us, we inflict suffering on ourselves and the rest of the world.

Shodo Harada urges us to "dig down" and "dig out" the illusory ego, to "get rid of the ego filter," through the rigorous practice of *zazen*. By persistent effort, he assures us, we can find that place where the "water of clear mind is flowing freely" and "the ego isn't directing our life." That is a high aspiration, requiring years of patient practice. But should that practice come to fruition, we may find ourselves less tethered to the "me-story," as Toni Packer has called it, and less inclined to divide "me" from "you" and "us" from "them." And should we find ourselves being tailgated on the Thruway, we may find that we no longer see a virtuous driver being bullied by a bad one. Rather, we see a field of rapidly changing relationships: a dangerous configuration of cars and drivers, to which that entity we call the self would do well to pay full attention.

8 March 2012

Consistency

Toward the end of the February 22 Republican primary debate, John King asked the candidates to define themselves in a single word. "Consistent," replied Representative Ron Paul. In the ensuing commentaries, Dr. Paul's response met with wide approval, even by those not partial to his views. "I'll give him that," Jon Stewart wryly remarked.

Ron Paul's response stood out from the others, not only because it came across as honest and accurate but also because it pointed toward his history rather than his temperament. Where the others laid claim to laudable traits of character—courage, resolution, cheerfulness—Ron Paul alluded to his public record. By so doing, he appealed to conventional wisdom, which holds that a candidate may best be judged by what he or she has said and done. "Ask me," wrote the American poet William Stafford, "if what I have done is my life." Under most circumstances, the answer would probably be yes. And should the next question be, "Who am I?" the standard of judgment might well be the same. The self exists in time, and a person may best be judged by examining his or her background, actions, and abiding traits of character. By such means we hire an employee or choose a doctor or pick a president.

Conventional wisdom can sometimes guide us, but it can also lead us astray. And if we stop and look deeply into the present moment, as Zen teachings enjoin us to do, we may find that conventional wisdom tells but half the story. Viewed from a conventional vantage point—what Zen calls that of "ordinary mind"—the conditioned self does indeed exist in time. It is born, lives, and dies. Concrete evidence may be found in our family albums, resumes, browsing histories, and countless other sources. But from the standpoint of what Zen calls "enlightened mind," which perceives a formless ground of being beneath the changing world of forms, the notion of a separate, historical self is seen to be a construct, a creation of the ego, which expends enormous energy in protecting its creation. "The past no longer is," the *Bhaddekaratta Sutra* reminds us. Ghosted though we are by our actions, statements, and previous relationships, our past has no tangible existence. Nor is a solid, permanent self anywhere to be found.

What *can* be found, according to Zen teachings, is an ever-changing aggregate of "form, feeling, thought, volition, and consciousness." Known in Zen as *skandhas*, these five elements comprise what we conventionally call the self. And the skandhas exist in a dynamic relationship, not only with each other but also with their environment, on which they depend for their continuing existence. Without sunlight, water, and fertile soil, the crocuses in our yard could not live for very long. Without the water, oxygen, minerals, and other nutrients we take from the natural world, neither could we. To imagine either the crocuses or ourselves to be separate entities, independent of changing surroundings, is to perpetuate a delusion. And to imagine a person as a kind of stone in a stream, impervious to the flux of conditions, is to ignore the impermanent, interdependent nature of both the self and its environment.

That is why, in Zen teachings, the entity we call the self is viewed in two disparate ways, as if through a stereoscope. Through one lens, as it were, the self is seen as the historical, time-bound form perceived by "ordinary mind." Like a wave on the ocean, it arises, endures, and expires. Through the other lens, however, the self is seen as the ocean itself: a timeless nexus of dynamic relationships, whose primary frame of reference is space rather than time. Viewed from the latter standpoint, what we normally call a person is understood, in the words of the psychologist Reginald Pawle, to be "an activity in relationship." And, as Pawle goes on to say, what we normally call a self is seen as a fluid being, whose consistency depends on its continuing awareness of its relationships:

> *Zen thought . . . asserts that continuity of self, psychological stability, occurs not over time, from the past to the future, but from continuing in relationship to one's situation, in the present, from continuing through space rather than time. Zen thought posits that a time-based self is a fragile self because time is always changing. From this perspective it can be said that space is what the self is, time is what the self is not.*

Seen in this perspective, the self remains continuous and stable only to the extent that it remains in touch with its environment, which is to say, with the changing conditions under which it continues to manifest. "I am what surrounds me," wrote the poet Wallace Stevens. By and large, Zen thought would agree, adding the proviso that to live in harmony with what surrounds us, we must remain present at all times. We must be fully awake.

This imperative has profound implications for the conduct of everyday life. It demands, first, that we remain ever-vigilant, ever aware of our conditioning, which would attach us both to our personal histories and to the illusion that things are solid and permanent when they are not. Beyond that, it demands that we remain acutely alert to changing conditions and our place within an unstable, unreliable environment, natural and social. Consistency matters, to be sure, as does that elusive factor known as character. But no less important is our capacity—or that of anyone who would be president—to respond, flexibly and compassionately, to whatever conditions may arise.

22 March 2012

Quiet Persistence

Are you an extrovert or an introvert? And if you happen to be the latter, how do you cope in a culture biased toward extroversion?

That is the central question posed by Susan Cain, a former corporate attorney, in her new book *Quiet: The Power of Introverts in a World That Can't Stop Talking*. According to studies cited by Cain, introverts make up thirty to fifty percent of the American population. Numbering herself among that cohort, Cain explores ways by which introverts can navigate a culture enthralled by what she calls the Extrovert Ideal. Those ways include adopting an extrovert's persona, creating a "restorative niche" in one's daily round, and negotiating respectfully with extroverted colleagues, friends, and spouses.

Beyond these practical stratagems, introverts can cultivate a quality Cain identifies as "soft power," or more specifically, "quiet persistence." Dramatically exemplified by Mahatma Gandhi, that quality is also a mark of traditional Asian culture, where habits of quiet study and attentive listening are encouraged and rewarded:

> *Soft power is not limited to moral exemplars like Mahatma Gandhi. Consider, for example, the much-ballyhooed excellence of Asians in fields like math and science. Professor [Preston] Ni defines soft power as "quiet persistence," and this trait lies at the heart of academic excellence as surely as it does in Gandhi's political triumphs. Quiet persistence requires sustained attention—in effect restraining one's reactions to external stimuli.*

As a case in point, Cain recounts the story of Tiffany Liao, a daughter of Taiwanese parents, whose habits of quiet study earned her admission to Swarthmore and an appointment as editor-in-chief of her college newspaper. Liao attributes her success to her "quiet traits," particularly her ability to listen attentively, take thorough notes, and do deep research prior to conducting interviews. In Cain's phrase, Liao came "to embrace the power of quiet," and that power enabled her to realize her dream.

For Tiffany Liao, as for introverts generally, quiet persistence may be a key to worldly success, but that quality of mind also has a place in the world's spiritual traditions, including Mahayana Buddhism, of which Zen is a late flowering. Mahayana teachings enjoin the practitioner to cultivate the six *paramitas* ("perfections of wisdom"). By doing so, the practitioner can eventually transform suffering and arrive at the "other shore" of wisdom and compassion. The six paramitas are generosity (*dana*), precepts (*sila*), patience (*kshanti*), diligence (*virya*), meditation (*samadhi*), and wisdom (*prajna*). "Quiet persistence" might be said to conflate two of the "perfections of wisdom," namely patience and diligence. This is a natural pairing, for the two qualities are both compatible and complementary.

The Sanskrit word *kshanti* is often translated as "patience." Other translations include "forbearance," "endurance," and "acceptance." Zen master Thich Nhat Hanh prefers the word "inclusiveness," which in his view comes closest to the original meaning:

> *Inclusiveness is the capacity to receive, embrace, and transform* . . . . *When we practice inclusiveness, we don't have to suffer or forbear, even when we have to embrace suffering and injustice. The other person says or does something that makes us angry. He inflicts on us some kind of injustice. But if your heart is large enough, we don't suffer* . . . . *To suppress our pain is not the teaching of inclusiveness. We have to receive it, embrace it, and transform it. The only way to do this is to make our heart big.*

In classical Zen teachings, practitioners of *kshanti paramita* are likened to the earth, which accepts all manner of impurities and toxins. Practicing *kshanti,* we include, without complaint, the pleasant with the unpleasant, the wholesome with the toxic, accepting and transforming it all in a spirit of compassion.

To some, that may sound like culpable passivity, especially if the adversity takes the form of an oppressive regime. But in Mahayana teachings, the paramitas do not exist in isolation, and *kshanti* is balanced by *virya paramita*, translated variously as "diligence," "perseverance," and "persistence." To practice *virya paramita* is to make a sustained, energetic effort. More precisely, it is to cultivate, with energy and persistence, such wholesome qualities as loving-kindness, compassion, sympathetic joy, and equanimity. As a practical technique, Thich Nhat Hanh urges us to keep the "energy of mindfulness" present as long as we can, once that energy has arisen. By the same token, we can decline to nourish such mental states as greed, envy, fear, and anger.

"Quiet persistence" shares common ground with the Japanese word *gaman*, which is rooted in Zen Buddhism and means "to be patient and persevere in the face of suffering," or, more simply, "to bear with it." By all accounts, the spirit of *gaman* was much in evidence in the aftermath of last year's earthquake and tsunami. Foreign correspondents described the long lines at gas stations and cash registers, where people waited patiently without complaint. Commentators noted the absence of looting and price-gouging and the willingness of people to help each other out. And since then, the world has watched the steady persistence of the Japanese in rebuilding their stricken country. As Nicholas Kristof has remarked, *gaman* is "steeped into the Japanese soul," and it may be indigenous to Japanese culture. But quiet persistence is a quality anyone can cultivate at any time, whether he or she be introverted or extroverted, traditional Asian or contemporary American.

5 April 2012

Wait Up!

It's a Saturday morning, and Jack and Ian are playing catch in their backyard. Jack is twelve, his brother ten. After they have tossed a softball back and forth for a while, Jack announces that he's going for a ride on his bike. Without waiting for a response, Jack mounts his bike and pedals off. "Wait up!" cries Ian, his older brother already far ahead.

Although Ian is probably unaware of it, he has just used a phrasal verb. In contrast to simple verbs, phrasal verbs contain two or more words, which function as a single semantic unit. "Wait up" differs in tone and meaning from "wait," and it also differs from "wait around" or "wait out." Phrasal verbs are a challenge for non-English speakers, who sometimes leave out the "particle"—the second word—or get it wrong. "I take my hat to you," a Japanese acquaintance once wrote to me, intending to offer a compliment but instead evoking an image of a vigorous assault.

In modern informal usage, *wait up* means "to stop or pause so that another can catch up" (*American Heritage Dic-*

tionary). Employed as an imperative, the phrase bears a distinctive tone, which can range from pleading to judgmental to mildly censorious. It implores the one who has forged ahead to slow down, pause, or stop. And it implies that the one who has gone ahead has been less than considerate of the one left behind.

Wait up might be a motto for the conduct of contemporary life. And it might also be a motto for Buddhist meditation, of which Zen is one variety. Buddhist meditation consists of two general processes, known respectively as *samatha* and *vipassana*. Usually translated as "stopping," *samatha* refers to concentrative meditation, which trains us to stop and pay attention to an object in the present, be it breathing or posture, a koan or a mantra. *Vipassana* is translated as "looking," or "looking with insight," and it employs the stability of mind generated by *samatha* to explore the nature of reality. In classical meditative training, "stopping" precedes "looking," the latter being sometimes described as the "harvest" of the former. But these two processes, however discrete, are understood to be aspects of a single practice.

"We have to learn the art of stopping," writes Thich Nhat Hanh, "stopping our thinking, our habit energies, our forgetfulness, the strong emotions that rule us. When an emotion rushes through us like a storm, we have no peace. We turn on the TV and then we turn it off. We pick up a book and then we put it down. How can we stop this state of agitation?"

One reliable way is to sit still and bring attention first to our breathing and then to parts of our bodies, silently reciting the verses, "Breathing in, I know I am breathing in / Breathing out, I know I am breathing out. // Aware of my eyes, I breathe in / Aware of my eyes, I breathe out." By employing this method and others like it, *samatha* practice calms our bodies, concentrates our minds, and heightens our awareness of our "habit energies," or patterns of habitual behavior. "All our life," wrote William James, "is but a mass of habits." Together those habits propel us into the future, often without our knowing it. *Samatha* puts the brakes on that powerful forward drive.

Yet for all its benefits *samatha* is also a limited practice, insofar as it focuses narrowly on the stability of the self. That is why *samatha* needs its complement *vipassana*, which trains the pacified mind to look into itself and examine the causes and conditions that have created its present state. If we are feeling angry, for example, we might discover that our anger stems from a friend's unkind remark. But if we look more deeply, we may recall that our friend's mother has recently been diagnosed with Alzheimer's disease. We might also find that both our propensity toward anger and our ways of managing it have roots in our family, our ancestry, and our culture.

In other words, by stopping and looking, we can become aware of our relationships, which in our rush to get ahead we may be leaving far behind. Many things can occasion that awareness, but the imperative "Wait up," posted above our desks or in some other conspicuous place, can be an especially potent reminder. It can halt our forward momentum and return us to the present moment. No less important, it can prompt us to examine those relationships that we may be neglecting, despite their importance in our lives.

Such was the case with an Honors student whom I will call Jessica, who took my college course in meditation some years ago. An anxious young woman, who was enrolled in twenty hours of courses while holding down two part-time jobs, Jessica discovered through the practice of meditation that she was living with a deep sense of loss and a habitual resentment toward her father. Toward the end of the semester, Jessica got in touch with her father, and over the next few weeks, they resolved much of their conflict. As Jessica's teacher, I found it instructive and heartening to observe how the simple practice of "stopping and looking"—or, if you like, of "waiting up"—could help to alleviate suffering and reconcile a daughter to her father.

19 April 2012

Timeless Flowers

*A*lthough the nights have been cold of late, the peonies in our perennial garden are energetically pushing up. Their crimson stalks are nearly knee-high; their white flowers will soon be in bloom. That is the nature of hardy perennials and the origin of their name: they come back every year. Having watched this happen, year after year, can we still greet the return of spring flowers with the excitement, joy, and awe we felt when we were younger?

That is the question addressed by two poems written in two very different times and places. The first is a *waka* by the Japanese poet Saigyo (1118-1190), a one-time samurai who became a wandering Buddhist monk:

Hana ni somu
kokoro no ika de
nokoriken
sute hateteki to
omou waga mi ni

—

Why should my heart
still harbor
this passion for cherry flowers,
I who thought
I had put all that behind me?

For anyone who has looked closely at cherry blossoms, whether in Kyoto or Washington, D.C., it may be hard to imagine *not* being moved by the flowers' evanescent beauty. What astonishes Saigyo, however, is his own response. A mature adult, he had thought his heart was jaded. Instead, he found his passion for natural beauty unabated.

Quite another perspective may be seen in "When We Were Children," a poem by the modern Irish poet Louis MacNeice (1915-1963):

When we were children words were colored
(Harlot and murder were dark purple)
And language was a prism, the light
    A conjured inlay on the grass,
Whose rays today are concentrated
    And language grown a burning-glass.

When we were children Spring was easy,
Dousing our heads in suds of hawthorn
And scrambling the laburnum tree—
    A breakfast for the gluttonous eye;
Whose winds and sweets have now forsaken
    Lungs that are black, tongues that are dry.

> *Now we are older and our talents*
> *Accredited to time and meaning,*
> *To handsel joy requires a new*
>   *Shuffle of cards behind the brain*
> *Where meaning shall remarry color*
>   *And flowers be timeless once again.*

Revisiting his childhood, MacNeice remembers a time when he experienced words as colors. *Harlot* and *murder*, words with dark connotations, were heard, read, and felt as the color purple. Words were wedded to the language of the senses, and language itself was experienced as a "prism"—a multicolored wonder rather than a tool of the concentrated mind.

Recalling the perceptions of his childhood, MacNeice also remembers its sensuous joys. Playing near a hawthorn bush or climbing a laburnum tree, he relished the scents and colors of the natural world, as if he were eating them for breakfast. Sadly, the middle-aged adult can no longer see, smell, or taste in quite the same way. Whether from smoking or some other cause, his lungs are black. His tongue no longer savors what it encounters. In an ironic reversal of agency, MacNeice attributes the loss of sensory acuity to the "winds and sweets" that have "forsaken" the aging narrator. In its absence, Spring is no longer "easy."

In his closing stanza, MacNeice returns to his central theme: the lost unity of language and the senses. A skeptical modernist with a keen awareness of history, MacNeice was well-accustomed to using analytic language in the service of "time and meaning." Yet he also found pleasure in the life of the senses, whether his subject was a bowl of roses in a bay window, seen against a background of snow, or a stream of images seen from a fast-moving train. Both as poet and literary intellectual, MacNeice endeavored to close the gap between word and thing, abstract concepts and the "incorrigibly plural" world of the senses, but as he acknowledges in his closing lines, that task requires a shift of orientation, a "shuffle of cards behind the brain."

For Saigyo, a poet-monk accustomed to the language and practice of non-duality, the direct apprehension of natural beauty may have come naturally. But for those of us who habitually divide subject from object, self from other, a direct encounter with natural phenomena is often impeded by language and dualistic thought, not to mention years of conditioning. "I must become a child again," wrote the poet Thomas Traherne. But in what way is one to do that? By what means may we rekindle and cultivate a sense of awe?

For the American essayist Scott Russell Sanders, one such way is the practice of bowing. In his essay "A Private History of Awe," Sanders recalls the recurrent experience, beginning in childhood, of losing all sense of a separate self. At such moments, "the fidgety self dissolves, as if it were a wave sliding back into the water, and there is only the swaying, shimmering sea." Now in his sixties, Sanders has come to realize that this experience of oneness, accompanied by a sense of awe, is "life's deepest truth." In keeping with that realization, he has made it a practice to sit in meditation every morning, trying only to be present, attentive, and open to whatever might occur. At the end of each sitting, Sanders rises, looks out at the waking world, and bows. This "little ritual," as he calls it, is a way of cultivating respect and reverence for "all that lives." It is also a way of honoring the "energy and glory in creation," which causes the cherry tree in his yard to break into bloom and the seeds in his garden to push toward the sun.

22 April 2012

Fixed Ideas

In a recent talk in Dublin, the Venerable Thich Nhat Hanh spoke of the happiness available to us in our everyday lives. We have only to "release our idea of happiness," he advised, and return to the present moment, where the conditions for happiness are already to be found.

Thich Nhat Hanh is not alone in offering this advice, nor is he unique in viewing ideas of happiness as obstacles to the experience itself. In his book *Beyond Happiness*, the Zen teacher Ezra Bayda deconstructs what he calls the "myth of happiness," which holds that "we deserve to be happy, as if it's our birthright; that we will be happy if we get what we want; that we can't be happy if we're in discomfort." For Bayda, as for Thich Nhat Hanh, our common human error lies in chasing an image of future happiness. Once we have shed that illusion, we can return "again and again to staying present with exactly what we are experiencing right now." Rather than try to manipulate our own or others' lives, we can "surrender to what is."

As can be inferred from the congruity of Thich Nhat Hanh's and Ezra Bayda's views, Zen teachings often remind us that happiness is to be found in the present moment, and that our notions of happiness, especially notions based on external conditions, only stand in our way. Yet in speaking of "releasing" our ideas of happiness, Thich Nhat Hanh has given this familiar teaching a fresh and energizing turn.

Derived from the Latin *relaxare* ("to relax"), the word release connotes freedom from confinement. Alternatively, it suggests the relinquishing of a right or claim. To speak of releasing our ideas of happiness is to suggest that we have been holding those ideas captive. We can let them go free. The word release also implies a claim to what Bayda would call a "birthright" or "sense of entitlement," which is to say, a right to be happy on our own terms. To release that claim is to liberate ourselves from the suffering that ensues when the claim proves illusory, the sense of entitlement a hindering fiction. By releasing our ideas of happiness, we open a path to genuine happiness, whose roots lie in a wholehearted, open-minded embracing of our lives as they are.

And just as our ideas of happiness can be released, so can our other ideas, especially those that may be causing harm. The Buddha famously said that the aim of all his teaching was the end of suffering. Elsewhere he declared that nothing whatsoever is to be clung to as "I" or "mine." The latter statement is sometimes understood to refer to material possessions, but it can also refer to our ideas, especially our fixed ideas, to which some of us cling at all costs, regardless of their tenuous connection to reality or their potential to inflict human suffering. To take but one example, there is the fixed idea of austerity, to which European governments have, until very recently, been clinging with all their might, against the best advice of Paul Krugman and other world-renowned economists. Whether that idea has been more toxic than beneficial is open to debate, but the tenacity of those who have embraced it has been self-evident.

To speak of clinging to ideas, economic or other, is not to denigrate thought or imply that thinking is inevitably linked to suffering. Without its ideas, the human mind would be a barren estate and the world a poorer place. What Zen teachings caution against is not intellection itself but our tendency to cherish and protect our ideas, as if they were private fortunes, and to identify with those ideas, as if *they* were *us*, and vice versa.

In reality, as the modern Zen master Kosho Uchiyama has put it, most of the ideas that cross our minds are as accidental as they are transient. To the extent that we are unaware of their comings and goings, we may view them as real and substantial—and fasten on them accordingly. By contrast, to the extent that we can live in awareness, we can see that our ideas, along with our memories, fantasies, and other mental phenomena, are no more solid than the chirp of a robin or the rumble of a passing truck. In a classic analogy from Zen teachings, our thoughts are likened to clouds in the sky—the sky-like nature of awareness. With practice we can learn to see them as such, while also observing our habitual clinging. In this way, we can, in Uchiyama's words, "open the hand of thought," releasing our pet ideas as if they were captive birds.

If you would like to test this proposition, may I suggest that you sit still in a comfortable, upright position and bring your awareness to your lower abdomen. Observe its rise as you breathe in, its fall as you breathe out. After a few minutes, shift your attention from your body to your mental life, and allow your awareness to illuminate your thoughts. Observe their arrival, duration, and departure. Note any tendency to pursue or cling to particular thoughts. At the same time, sense your capacity to release your thoughts, even those you most value. Practice this ten-minute exercise daily for a week or more, and see what becomes of your fixed ideas.

16 May 2012

Watch What You're Doing

"Watch, watch, watch what your doin'," chanted Bob Marley at the One Love Peace Concert in Kingston, Jamaica in 1978. At the time, Jamaica was torn by sectarian violence, and Marley had returned from London in the hope of promoting reconciliation. Hearing Marley's improvised chant, the crowd of 32,000 assumed he was voicing a general warning. *Watch what you're doing*, lest you cause further harm.

As it happened, Marley was speaking to Junior Marvin, his lead guitarist, who had just played a wrong note. "Everybody thought he was telling the people out there you gotta watch what you're doin'," Marvin recalls in Kevin Macdonald's documentary *Marley*, "but he was really talking to *me*." Given Marley's stature as a moral leader, it is understandable that his audience might interpret his words as a cautionary exhortation. But their actual context was immediate and professional, their intent practical rather than prophetic.

What happened to Bob Marley's words on that evening has also happened to those of the old Zen masters, whose paradoxical *obiter dicta*, cryptic *non sequiturs*, and enigmatic pronouncements have been interpreted many times over in subsequent commentaries. Over the centuries, what was said in a specific cultural context has often been elevated to the level of a universal. What was contingent has become proverbial. The result is sometimes a gain in resonance, as words uttered in a particular time and place become words to live by. But in the process, the contexts and concrete circumstances of the masters' words have sometimes been minimized—or forgotten altogether.

Here, for example, is a famous Zen koan, known to Zen students as "Joshu's 'Wash your Bowl'":

> *A monk said to Joshu, "I have just entered this monastery. Please teach me."*
> *"Have you eaten your rice porridge?" asked Joshu.*
> *"Yes, I have," replied the monk.*
> *"Then you had better wash your bowl."*
> *With this, the monk gained insight.*

In this story, a novice monk asks the renowned Zen master Joshu (Ch. *Zhaozhou*, 778-897), from whose lips light was said to come forth, to teach him the practice of Zen. Rather than answer, Joshu asks a question, followed by an imperative: "wash your bowl." That imperative could hardly be plainer, but it is also open to interpretation. What, exactly, did Joshu mean, or mean to imply? What insight did the monk attain?

In his commentary on "Wash Your Bowl," Katsuki Sekida (1903-1987), a Soto lay teacher and respected translator of the classic koans, provides some helpful information. As

Sekida explains, the meal to which Joshu refers is the morning meal of hot rice porridge, which Zen monks are expected to eat in a state of *samadhi*, or one-pointed concentration. Having eaten his breakfast in samadhi, the monk has already experienced the practice of Zen, although he may not have realized it at the time. Now he should wash his bowl in the same spirit. At once Socratic and direct, Joshu's teaching hits the mark, and the monk gains insight into the practice he has entered.

Yet, as Sekida notes, Joshu's admonition is also a "Zen proverb." Informed though it is by its monastic context, it is not dependent on that context. As Sekida observes, "[i]n samadhi every moment is independent, cut off before and behind. The monk is no longer at breakfast; he should pay attention to the present. What is past is past: wash it away, good or evil." Framed in this fashion, "Wash your bowl" resembles other Zen proverbs, such as "Every day is a good day" or "The elbow does not bend outward." Like such Western counterparts as "haste makes waste," Zen proverbs do not require a supporting historical context. They can stand alone, and they can be invoked wherever they might apply.

That is demonstrably true of "Wash your Bowl," but it is fair to say that if this story is stripped of its original setting, it loses much of its character and color. In Zen monasteries and centers, ancient and modern, the washing of one's eating bowls is viewed as a sacred ritual. During extended retreats, Zen practitioners eat three silent, formal meals a day. At the end of each, they wash, stack, and wrap their eating bowls at the table, following an elaborate protocol. Dating from the time of Eihei Dogen (1200-1253), this traditional protocol is meticulously observed and strictly enforced. Washing one's bowl is seen as an act of veneration, an expression of gratitude, and an occasion to contemplate the emptiness of self. To reduce "Wash your Bowl" to a sagacious proverb, omitting its monastic context, is to leave out this spiritual dimension, diminishing both the story and its meaning.

Fortunately, it is not really a matter of either/or. "Wash your bowl" can be interpreted and applied at both the proverbial and literal levels. Understanding Joshu's admonition as a proverb, we can apply it to any activity that involves washing, cleaning, or otherwise removing toxins and impurities. We can even extend its compass to include the cleansing of our minds: the removal of such mental pollutants as worrying, fantasizing, and unnecessary judging of people and things. But by recalling the literal context of "Wash your Bowl" and its connection to formal monastic meals, we can remind ourselves that we don't have to be rushed, careless, or distracted, either while we eat or while we perform what the British call "washing up." On the contrary, with practice we can eat our meals and wash our dishes with gratitude, full awareness, and the utmost care. Moment by moment, we can watch what we are doing.

30 May 2012

Mudita and Social Media

If you spend much time on Facebook, you may have noticed the response that so often follows an announcement of personal achievement. "Congratulations!" exclaims a respondent, sometimes within minutes of the announcement. "That's wonderful," writes another. "We're very happy for you," declares a third. If the achiever's circle of Facebook friends numbers in the hundreds or even thousands, the roster of congratulants may extend to thirty or more, creating a visible avalanche of affirmation, a collective expression of unselfish joy.

Such expressions are common at weddings, graduations, and other real-life occasions, but their virtual presence on Facebook is something new. At the same time, it is something very old, insofar as it resembles a state of mind known to Buddhist practitioners as *mudita*, or "sympathetic joy." One of the four "immeasurable minds" (*brahminviharas*) of Buddhist teachings, mudita may be defined as the capacity to feel and express joy in someone else's happiness or success. Like the other "immeasurable minds"—loving-kindness, compassion, and equanimity—mudita is both a mind-state and a practice. It is to be contemplated and cultivated on a daily basis. And, as the Buddhist scholar C.F. Knight has noted, mudita "multiplies in ratio to the extension of its application, quite apart from its purifying effect on our own lives." Yet, unlike the other "immeasurable minds," mudita is seldom discussed in the meditative community. And should one venture to bring it up outside that community, one must be prepared to encounter raised eyebrows, looks of puzzlement, or even tacit derision. Cultivate sympathetic joy? Feel joy at others' success? You must be joking.

If mudita goes largely unexamined in meditative circles, and if its mention is greeted with skepticism in the culture at large, it may be because sympathetic joy is a difficult emotion to identify or validate, much less put into practice. Ours is a competitive society. Do we honestly feel unalloyed joy when someone succeeds, especially if his or her enterprise is similar to our own? Do we not feel a trace of envy as well—or secretly begrudge a colleague's success? "It is relatively easier," writes Nyanaponika Thera, "for man to feel compassion or friendliness in situations which demand them, than to cherish a spontaneous feeling of shared joy, outside a narrow circle of one's family and friends." And, as Natasha Jackson notes, it is "a depressing fact that people are much more ready to sympathize with the misfortunes of others than to rejoice with them." To do so requires genuine affection, first for the object of unselfish joy, and second, for humankind itself. If you are a bitter misanthrope, you are unlikely to feel mudita, even if your favorite uncle has just won the lottery. That's nice, all right, but why couldn't you have won it yourself?

To gain a deeper appreciation of mudita, it is helpful to contrast it with its "far enemies," as they are called in Buddhist texts, and with its polar opposite. The far enemies of mudita are jealousy and envy, the noxious weeds that sympathetic joy is supposed to expunge. But its polar opposite is *schadenfreude*, a state of mind memorably described by the French courtier La Rochefoucauld (1613-1680): *Dans l'adversité de nos meilleurs amis nous trouvons quelque chose qui ne nous déplaît pas.* ("In the misfortunes of our best friends we always find something not altogether displeasing"). In his "Verses on the Death of Dr. Swift"(1731), the author of *Gulliver's Travels* takes La Rochefoucauld's maxim as his theme, as he reflects on the ubiquity of envy:

> *We all behold with envious eyes,*
> *Our equal raised above our size;*
> *Who would not at a crowded show,*
> *Stand high himself, keep others low?*
> *I love my friend as well as you*
> *But would not have him stop my view;*

Having thus established his context, Swift turns from the subject of envy to the prospect of his own death:

> *Then he who prophesied the best,*
> *Approves his foresight to the rest:*
> *You know, I always feared the worst*
> *And often told you so at first:*
> *He'd rather choose that I should die,*
> *Than his prediction prove a lie.*

What animates his so-called friends, Swift concludes, is not sympathy for a dying man's pain but the egoistic pleasure of predicting the time of his death.

For those who share Jonathan Swift's vision, mudita may seem an ineffectual antidote. Like beauty in Shakespeare's 65th sonnet, its action is no stronger than a flower. Yet, as its virtual presence on Facebook vividly confirms, mudita is not an idealist's fanciful notion. It too has a place in human affairs, and it too can be cultivated, once the reality of interconnectedness has been embraced, and the fiction of a separate self has been set aside. To be sure, the version of mudita posted on Facebook is a digital facsimile, a static simulacrum of the living thing. But it is probably no accident that it should appear on a social network, where evidence of interconnectedness is everywhere to be found. As my son, Alexander Howard, recently remarked in a public forum, social media provide a venue for "looking at things together," whether the object of scrutiny be an atrocity in Syria, a photo of a newborn child, or a cache of government data. And it would be a salutary development if a medium sometimes viewed as a vehicle for self-concern should become a seedbed for mudita and a locus of a long-neglected virtue.

13 June 2012

The Cliché Monster

For many years I taught courses in imaginative writing to college students, and when it came time to read their work, I kept three tools of the trade close at hand.

One was a fine-point pen, with which I corrected errors of grammar and usage. Another was a mechanical pencil, with which I made marginal comments. And the third was a small rubber stamp, which fit neatly into its circular ink pad. A relic of my son's childhood, the stamp produced a miniature image of a Tyrannosaurus Rex, complete with oversized head, upraised tail, and greedy-looking paws. At once fierce and benign in aspect, this creature was known as the Cliché Monster, and whenever a cliché appeared in a student's essay, poem, or story, he too would appear, poised to devour the offending phrase. "Don't feed him," I warned the students, "or he'll come back for more."

As might be expected, a few students ignored that warning or took it as a dare, teasing or testing the Monster with intentional clichés. But most understood that this silly little figure had a serious role to play in their education. Broadly speaking, the Cliché Monster engendered awareness of the tendency, common to us all, to write, think, and even feel in clichés. More subtly, his presence made novice writers aware of the difference between a common English idiom, which might add a conversational flavor to a sentence, and an outright verbal cliché, which is to language and thought what dead cells are to the skin. To say, for example, that you're at your wit's end is to enlist an admissible, if rather tired, idiom. But to say that you're "at the end of [your] tether" is to emit the scent of cliché and invite a visit from the Monster. And to write (or say) that someone should "step up to the plate," or worse, that one or another political party is "kicking the can down the road," is to offer the Cliché Monster a meal of prime red meat, a verbal feast of clichéd perception.

As has often been noted, the practices of writing and Zen have much in common, and nowhere is their common ground more evident than in this issue of freshness. Many years ago, in a public interview, an unsuccessful candidate for the presidency of Alfred University observed that "we have to have a cushion in case there's a ripple in the admissions picture." I took note of that remark, not only because it was a masterpiece of mixed metaphor but also because it entirely befogged the candidate's meaning. What he meant to say, I eventually discerned, was that the university needed to have funds in reserve in the event that enrollment dropped. But his conceptual language, being a tissue of clichéd metaphors, stood between the listener and the import of the speaker's words.

As proponents of clarity and vivacity in the use of language, teachers of composition disdain clichés chiefly because they dull the student's work and tend to obscure its meaning. From the vantage point of Zen teachings, however, clichés are to be avoided because they exemplify, in extreme form, the propensity of conceptual language to mask the reality it purports to illuminate. Readers of this column may remember that its title refers to the Japanese motto *ichigo ichie*, which is closely associated with the tea ceremony and is usually translated as "one time, one meeting." As this motto asserts, each meeting of host and guests in the tea hut is unprecedented and unrepeatable. However governed by custom and tradition, each is a once-in-a-lifetime experience. And what is true of the tea ceremony, Zen teachings tell us, is also true of our experience generally. By relying upon clichéd language, we deny the "suchness" of each new experience. To call a landscape "breathtaking" is not only to be less than fresh in one's thought and expression. It is also to overlook the particulars of that particular landscape—or ignore its uniqueness altogether. Having placed the mountain or glacier or fjord in the category of Breathtaking Landscapes, we may cease to see it afresh.

At the same time, we may also cease to recognize its impermanence, its ever-changing nature. "Practitioners have always understood impermanence as the cornerstone of Buddhist teachings and practice," notes the Zen priest Zoketsu Norman Fischer. "[N]othing lasts. Therefore nothing can be grasped or held onto." At their most banal, clichés are the by-products of laziness or haste: we can't be bothered or don't have the time to see things as they are or describe them accordingly. But at their most pernicious, clichés are also gestures toward an illusory sense of permanence: efforts to grasp and make solid what is actually fluid and dynamic. Originally, the word cliché referred to a printer's stereotype: an oft-used phrase cast on a metal plate. A practical convenience, the cliché spared the printer time and energy. That was good for the printer—but not so good for those who might wish, in the words of the poet Patrick Kavanagh, to "snatch out of time the passionate transitory."

Nowadays most printing is done by computer, and the printer's cliché is no longer in service. But clichés themselves are *alive and well*, as a glance at a newspaper or an hour spent watching *Meet the Press* will readily verify. And though I have long since retired the Cliché Monster, I have thought it advisable to keep his mental counterpart in close proximity, especially when writing prose or verse. Like Hemingway's famous "BS detector," that little dinosaur has a job to do.

27 June 2012

Just Say "Oh"

One evening last month, I took my young friend Isabel on a walk past our flower garden. Isabel is three years old. As we walked along, I named the flowers she was seeing: *Wisteria. Coleus. Viola. Geranium.* Isabel stooped to inspect the geranium, whose bright red petals had caught her eye.

Not long afterward, Isabel and I arrived at our deck, where my father-in-law, Saul, was relaxing in his wheelchair. An 89-year-old veteran of World War Two, Saul wears a full white beard, and he is seldom seen without his blue, *U.S.S. Hornet* cap. "Isabel," said my wife, Robin, "This is my dad, Mr. Caster."

Isabel looked up at Saul quizzically, as though he might be another, somewhat larger flower. "Why are you in a wheelchair?" she asked.

"Because I only have one leg," Saul replied.

"Oh," said Isabel, taking a moment to absorb that information. "Very nice to meet you," she said, extending her hand.

Isabel soon dashed off to play with a friend, but her response left a lasting impression, not least because it was so unfiltered. It evinced a capacity to meet the external world, including its unfamiliar and potentially disturbing aspects, with openness, curiosity, and an absence of comment.

Many children possess that capacity, and some adults manage to retain it. But it can also be cultivated through the practice of Zen meditation. In *The Way of Zen* Alan Watts offers this description of the practice:

> *To see the world as it is concretely, undivided by categories and abstractions, one must certainly look at it with a mind which is not thinking—which is to say, forming symbols—about it.* Zazen [seated meditation] *is not, therefore, sitting with a blank mind which excludes all the impressions of the inner and outer senses. It is not "concentration" in the usual sense of restricting the attention to a single sense object . . . . It is simply a quiet awareness, without comment, of whatever happens to be here and now.*

Essential to this description is the phrase "without comment." To be aware of realities while making comments or forming judgments about them is one thing. To cultivate a quiet awareness of those same realities, *without comment*, is quite another.

It may be asked why intelligent adults with well-stocked minds would wish to eschew comment. Every day most of us consume huge volumes of information, and as Clay Johnson observes in his book *The Information Diet,* a disproportionate amount of what we consume is commentary, especially commentary with which we agree. In a world without comment, Shields and Brooks would soon be out of a job, as would

Rachel Maddow, Sean Hannity, and a host of others. Moreover, our cultural history would be denuded of most of its proverbs, jokes, retorts, and memorable remarks. Comment, it might be said, is the stuff of life. Why would we wish to discourage it, much less embrace a practice that endeavors to exclude it? And why would Zen teachings, which themselves abound in commentary, encourage such a practice?

To begin with, from the standpoint of Zen teachings, comment is often superfluous. "The Way," writes Seng-ts'an in the *Faith-Mind* sutra, "is perfect as vast space is perfect, / where nothing is lacking and nothing is in excess." Undifferentiated reality is perfect, complete, and "beyond language." It requires no comment from us. Therefore we should "cease attachment to talking and thinking" and not waste our time in arguments, "attempting to grasp the ungraspable." Although Seng-ts'an is speaking of absolute reality rather than our relative, historical existence, his advice has a bearing on ordinary life. Having just experienced a moment of elation or sorrow or transcendent beauty, do we really need to comment? What, if anything, do our comments add?

And what, we might also ask, do they subtract? Language is by nature dualistic. Words in general and comments in particular include certain aspects of the realities we perceive while leaving others out. "'Holiness,'" writes Thich Nhat Hanh, "is only the word 'holiness.' And when we say the word 'holiness,' we eliminate everything that isn't holy, like the ordinary.... When we say a name out loud, it is as if we are slashing a knife into reality and cutting it into small pieces." In similar fashion, Witold Pilecki, a Polish Army officer who survived Auschwitz, writes of those who did not, "To be honest, can I write that someone was 'much missed'?

I missed them all." In short, to say one thing is not to say another—and to risk falsifying the reality one purports to record.

Beyond these redundant and reductive aspects of commentary, there is also its propensity to preempt experience itself. By their nature comments are indicative rather than interrogative. They express what the speaker already knows. Useful as that may be, it can also abort an experience even before it has occurred. By refraining from comment, we can cultivate the state of mind Zen calls "not-knowing," which is at once a well of creativity and a humbling alternative to speech. "Even brief silence," writes the physicist George Prochnik in his book *In Pursuit of Silence*, "can inject us with a fertile unknown: a space in which to focus and absorb experience . . . a reflection that some things we cannot put into words are yet resounding real."

So what, in the presence of the new and strange, are we to do? Perhaps, for once, we might remain silent. We might cultivate what Buddhism calls "bare attention," an awareness of body and mind prior to judgment or comment. Or, if we wish to emulate Isabel, we might just say, "Oh."

11 July 2012

Noble Silence

In Philip Larkin's celebrated poem "Church Going," a secular Englishman, out for a ride on his bicycle, stops at a local parish church. After making sure that "there's nothing going on," he steps inside, casting a cool but observant eye on what he encounters:

> Another church: matting, seats, and stone,
> And little books; sprawlings of flowers, cut
> For Sunday, brownish now; some brass and stuff
> Up at the holy end; the small neat organ;
> And a tense, musty, unignorable silence,
> Brewed God knows how long. Hatless, I take off
> My cycle-clips in awkward reverence . . .

As can be seen from these perceptions, Larkin's narrator is ill at ease in his surroundings. They are musty and make him tense. Yet, as he will inform us later on, he was drawn to this "cross of ground" and its "unignorable" silence. And though he summons an ironic phrase ("up at the holy end") to bolster his resistance, he attempts a gesture of respect.

"Church Going" was written in 1954. Since that time, the personal and cultural ambivalence the poem embodies has grown ever more acute. On the one hand, there is our culture's collective yearning, widely felt and frequently expressed, for silence and silent spaces. On the other, there is our seemingly inexhaustible will, enabled by cell phones, mobile devices, and other components of advanced technology, to resist, avoid, or destroy whatever silence remains. We want to be silent, it would seem, but we no longer know how.

In his book *In Pursuit of Silence* the physicist George Prochnik examines this ambivalence, giving a fair hearing to either side. His wide-ranging exploration leads him to the New Melleray Abbey, a Trappist monastery in northeastern Iowa, where he experiences the soundlessness of an underground chapel, and on to the Portland Japanese Garden, where raked white gravel represents emptiness and silence. But Prochnik also investigates the engineered "soundscapes" of restaurants and stores, the "harmonic relations in infant cries," and, at the furthest extreme, a "boom car" "boom-off" in Tampa, Florida, where enthusiasts of loudness compete with their woofers to shatter the windshields of their cars. Throughout his auditory journey, Prochnik maintains his objectivity, balancing his love of silence with his interest in all things acoustic. But in the end he is led to conclude that as a culture we are experiencing an "epidemic of excessive acoustical stimulation," whose impact on our health and sanity may be far more damaging than we've realized. Noise is "defiantly on the rise." If we truly want silence, we must build spaces that create and protect it.

For centuries Zen monasteries, like their Trappist counterparts, have endeavored to do just that. Josh Swiller, a former Buddhist monk, has described Buddhist meditation as "the study of silence," and for the most part the daily life of a Zen monastery is tailored to that purpose. Idle chat is discouraged. Talk is kept to a functional minimum. And during the extended retreats known as *sesshin*, a code of silence is strictly enforced. Among the benefits of this "noble silence," as it is called, are the conservation of energy, the replenishment of the senses, and the realization that speech, when not overtly harmful, is often redundant. And, as I learned from my own experience at Dai Bosatsu Zendo, a Rinzai Zen monastery in the Catskills, the noble silence of monastic life can also provide insights into the nature of sound, whether its source be external or internal.

Silence and sound are sometimes thought of as polarities, but they might better be seen as points on a continuum. Silence is a matter of degree. And within the relative silence of the monastery, such sounds as do occur are often starkly amplified. Like black dots on a vast white canvas, they take on an unwonted magnitude.

So it was one morning at Dai Bosatsu, when a few of us were sitting in our robes in the dimly-lit *zendo*. Streams of early light shimmered on the dark oak floor. All was quiet and still. And then, abruptly, the *jikijitsu* broke the prevailing silence. "Breathe silently!" he barked. "If I can hear you breathing, it's too loud!" Duly admonished, we resumed our *zazen*. But not long afterward, we learned that our vigilant jikijitsu had missed the mark. What he had heard as audible breathing was in fact a porcupine, rustling in the bushes outside the open door.

Beyond such external sounds, there is also the noise our minds are making. Whether its specific content be memories or fantasies, judgments or speculations, that egocentric racket is more or less continuous, and it becomes especially pronounced in the silence of the zendo. In a teaching entitled "This Silence is Called Great Joy," Thich Nhat Hanh quotes a classic Buddhist verse:

> *All formations are impermanent.*
> *They are subject to birth and death.*
> *But remove the notions of birth and death,*
> *and this silence is called great joy.*

As Thich Nhat Hanh explains, the first two lines of this verse remind us that all things come and go. They are born and die. But the last two lines make a counter-assertion, which is that dualistic notions—impermanence and permanence, birth and death, sound and silence—can be removed. Through the diligent practice of zazen they can be released, leaving us in the silence of absolute reality. In Buddhist teachings, silence of this kind is known as *nirvana*, which means, among other things, "the extinction of all notions," especially notions of self and other. Should we be fortunate enough to experience this deeper silence, Zen teachings promise, and should we manage to maintain it in our daily round, it will bring great joy, whether we happen to be sitting zazen, or visiting an empty parish church, or enduring the ignoble noise of contemporary life.

8 August 2012

This World Uncertain Is

Of what may we be certain? In the vast cosmos, as in our circumscribed private lives, what is predictable and what is not? Between the expected and the unexpected, where does the balance lie?

Some fifty years ago, in an essay entitled "The Unexpected Universe," the distinguished anthropologist Loren Eiseley (1907-1977) eloquently addressed those questions. Recalling a remark by the nineteenth-century German scientist Heinrich Hertz, who believed that "knowledge of nature" would enable us to predict future events and arrange our present affairs accordingly, Eiseley contrasted Hertz's confident outlook with that of a previous era:

> *Hertz's remark seems to offer surcease from uncertainty, power contained, the universe understood, the future apprehended before its emergence. The previous Elizabethan age, by contrast, had often attached to its legal documents a humble obeisance to life's uncertainties expressed in the*

> *phrase "by the mutability of fortune and favor." The men of Shakespeare's century may have known less of science, but they knew only too well what unexpected overthrow was implied in the frown of a monarch or a breath of the plague.*

Among the many resonant phrases in this passage, one in particular stands out. In speaking of a "humble obeisance to life's uncertainties," Eiseley evokes the courtly manners of Elizabethan England. Beyond that, he invokes an outlook as foreign to our own time as Shakespeare's diction is to contemporary English.

For centuries the world's great spiritual traditions, Zen Buddhism included, have warned against pride and encouraged humility. Pride goeth before destruction. The meek shall inherit the earth. In classical Zen teachings, however, pride and humility are rarely discussed in terms of sin or virtue. Rather, they are understood to be the symptoms, respectively, of ignorance and awakening. "Form is emptiness, emptiness form," the *Heart Sutra* tells us: the form we call the self is empty of a separate, intrinsic existence. Like a wave on the ocean or a whirlpool in a stream, the self exists, but it is no more solid than it is immutable. To be proud of that contingent self, to imagine its being apart from and superior to the stream of life, is to harbor a foolish notion and often to bring harm upon oneself and others. Yet the root cause of suffering lies not in self-pride but in what Buddhism calls a fundamental ignorance of reality. And contrariwise, the realization (through the practice of meditation) of the emptiness of self fosters a humbler view of one's place in the world. Meditation engenders wisdom, and wisdom engenders humility.

To cultivate the wisdom of humility, of course, is not necessarily to embrace obeisance. The word obeisance, which derives from "obey" and refers to such gestures as bows and curtsies, has become rare if not archaic. And so has the concept itself, insofar as it connotes deference to a human authority. In Zen practice, a kind of obeisance is expressed through the bow known as *gassho*, palms pressed together, and especially through prostrations, which constitute an integral part of Zen liturgy. For many people bows present no particular problem, but even committed Zen practitioners sometimes resist the formal prostration, forehead touching the floor, which the fourteenth-century Zen master Bassui Tokusho described as "a way of horizontalizing the mast of ego in order to realize the Buddha-nature." No less an adept than Philip Kapleau Roshi, founder of the Rochester Zen Center, described how much he resisted prostrating himself before his Japanese teacher during his first formal interview. "How that went against my grain," he recalled, "and how I resisted it! Why should I bow down before another human being?" Sometime later, having sensed his student's resistance, Kapleau's teacher explained that in performing a prostration Kaplaeu was bowing not to his teacher but to his own "Buddha-nature." That "revelation," Kapleau reported, resolved his dilemma. And later, as a teacher himself, he fully endorsed the practice of prostrations. "When entered into sincerely," he contended, "[they] are a source of spiritual nourishment that everyone, awakened or not, can tap."

Perhaps so. But if, as denizens of a democratic, individualistic culture, we can manage to bow to our better natures, can we also bow to "life's uncertainties"? To borrow a phrase from Alan Watts, can we embody the wisdom of insecurity?

Toward that end Zen teachings offer a practice called "not-knowing," or, in its Korean formulation, "Don't-know mind." In this practice we sit still, become aware of our breathing, and repeatedly ask the question, "What is this?" followed by the statement "I don't know." By so doing, we cut through easy answers and habitual responses, becoming ever more intimate with the present reality. Simultaneously, we train ourselves to accept uncertainty and its attendant anxiety.

Not-knowing" is a difficult practice under any circumstances, but it is especially so when transported from the meditation hall into the uncertainties of everyday life. It is one thing to contemplate the idea of "life's uncertainties" on the meditation cushion. It is quite another to do so while waiting for the results of a biopsy or a loved one's MRI. Yet over time, the practice of "not-knowing" can fortify us against such crises, in the same way that a muscle can be strengthened through physical training.

"This world uncertain is," wrote the Elizabethan poet Thomas Nashe in "A Litany in Time of Plague" (1600). For those who believe that everything happens for a reason, or that a wise and munificent deity governs the universe, the fact framed by Nashe's line may be easier to bear. Absent such consolations, however, the line itself can be a salutary mantra. Posted above one's desk or installed in a mobile device, it can remind us that uncertainty is an inescapable part of the human condition. In the words of the Vipassana teacher Jack Kornfield, it can prompt us to "bow to what is."

22 August 2012

True Equanimity

One morning earlier this summer, I found myself standing atop an unstable blue object known as a BOSU Ball. Invented by David Weck in 1999, the BOSU Balance Trainer is an inflatable rubber hemisphere attached to a rigid platform. The central component of a "mindful approach to exercise," the BOSU Ball is designed to improve the body's sense of balance while strengthening its stabilizing muscles. I was standing on the BOSU Ball because I'd been having knee pain, and our family doctor had recommended physical therapy. In turn, the affable but exacting physical therapist with whom I was working had prescribed the BOSU Ball. "Don't fall off," he cheerfully warned, having just assigned me thirty squats. Miraculously, I managed to comply.

In a manner analogous to that of the BOSU Ball, Zen practice also aims to strengthen our sense of balance, physical and emotional. In Zen teachings, the capacity to maintain one's equilibrium, especially under stressful, uncertain, and unstable conditions, is known as *equanimity*, a translation of the Sanskrit word *upeksha*. The traditional posture of sitting meditation—knees down, back erect, head balanced on the spine—supports the cultivation of *upeksha,* as does the practice of walking meditation, which trains the practitioner to walk with dignity and steady awareness. But these forms and practices, however essential to Zen discipline, are but the outward expressions of an inner poise. And at the heart of that inner poise is a balanced, inclusive way of experiencing the world.

In his explanation of *upeksha*, Zen master Thich Nhat Hanh examines the roots of the term and its deeper implications:

> [Upeksha] *means equanimity, nonattachment, nondiscrimination, even-mindedness, or letting go.* Upa *means "over," and* iksh *means "to look." You climb the mountain to be able to look over the whole situation, not bound by one side or the other. If your love has attachment, discrimination, prejudice, or clinging in it, it is not true love. People who do not understand Buddhism sometimes think upeksha means indifference, but true equanimity is neither cold nor indifferent. If you have more than one child, they are all your children. Upeksha does not mean that you don't love. You love in a way that all your children receive your love, without discrimination.*

As is evident from this explanation, the word equanimity means more than remaining calm under pressure, though calm is a part of it. True equanimity is grounded in a fundamental opening of the heart and mind. It arises from and is sustained by a radically egalitarian social attitude.

Upeksha is one of four such attitudes in Buddhist teachings, the other three being loving-kindness (*metta*), compassion (*karuna*), and sympathetic joy (*mudita*). Known as the Four Immeasurable Minds, these attitudes may be developed through daily, systematic practice. Specific methods vary according to content, but their general form remains essentially the same. We begin by focusing on ourselves (*"May I be balanced and at peace"*) and from there proceed to address a loved one, an acquaintance, a stranger, an enemy, and "all sentient beings." Simplifying that sequence, Pema Chodron recommends, for equanimity, a three-stage recitation: "May I dwell in the great equanimity free from passion, aggression, and prejudice. May you dwell in the great equanimity free from passion, aggression, and prejudice. May all beings enjoy the great equanimity free from passion, aggression, and prejudice." "It is always fine," she adds, "to use your own words."

It is indeed fine–and perhaps preferable—to use one's own words, but where equanimity is concerned, we must also be careful not to misinterpret the quality we are attempting to cultivate. As Thich Nhat Hanh notes above, true equanimity is not a cold indifference to others' suffering. Nor is equanimity a passive, see-no-evil neutrality. As the Zen teacher Norman Fischer puts it, equanimity is an "active, loving, eyes-wide-open regard for all beings—equally." The practice of equanimity does not oblige us to regard Hitler and Neville Chamberlain as moral equivalents—or, to take a contemporary example, to view the actions of Bashar Al-Assad and his political opponents as equally culpable. What it does demand is that we remain, in Fischer's words, "fully present, fully alive, right in the middle of things," and that we meet even the most adverse situation with a warm, calm, and balanced attitude. Far from encouraging a callous detachment or false neutrality, the practice of equanimity fosters empathy for our fellow human beings, including those we most dislike, while allowing us to retain our personal integrity.

For most of us, that is a formidable challenge, but the potential rewards are no less considerable. In Buddhist teachings, equanimity is regarded as the highest of the Four Immeasurable Minds. It is said to perfect and consummate the other three. The American Buddhist monk Bhikkhu Bodhi describes equanimity as "a state of inner equipoise that cannot be upset by gain and loss, honor and dishonor, praise and blame, pleasure and pain." Brought to fruition in the fullness of time, equanimity establishes an "unshakeable freedom of mind," emancipating the practitioner from "all points of self-reference" and "the demands of the ego-self," which tug us this way and that. No longer in thrall to those demands, we come to embody what Thich Nhat Hanh has called the "wisdom of non-discrimination," which dissolves prejudicial attitudes and removes erected boundaries between ourselves and others. Should we eventually attain that wisdom, we will not only have restored our sense of balance and secured our emotional footing. We will also have brought a humane, equanimous perspective into our everyday lives.

5 September 2012

Resting in the Immediate

In a poem entitled "The Little Duck," the American philosopher Donald C. Babcock (1886-1986) depicts a duck riding the Atlantic "a hundred feet beyond the surf":

This is some sort of duck, and he cuddles in the swells.
He isn't cold, and he is thinking things over.
There is a big heaving in the Atlantic,
And he is part of it.
He looks a bit like a mandarin, or the Lord Buddha meditating under the Bo tree,
But he has hardly enough above the eyes to be a philosopher.
He has poise, however, which is what philosophers must have.

Closely observing his subject, Babcock notes that the duck "can rest while the Atlantic heaves, because he rests in the Atlantic." And though the duck "probably doesn't *know* how large the ocean is," he "*realizes* it, and he "sits down in it." He "reposes in the immediate as if it were infinity—which it is."

To compare a sitting duck, however poised, to the Lord Buddha may seem an irreverent stretch, but Babcock's characterization of the duck's action—or non-action—as reposing in the immediate accurately describes one form of Zen meditation. Known as *shikantaza*, or "just sitting," this practice is central to the Soto Zen tradition and is often regarded as the purest form of Zen meditation. Rather than count breaths, probe a koan, or otherwise engage in concentrative mental activity, the practitioner of shikantaza brings an open, panoramic attention to whatever is occurring in the present moment. Rather than filter experience through concepts and their emotional colorations, he or she rests in a quiet, unmediated awareness.

That may sound easy, and for a wild duck it may be so. But for most people it takes sustained, disciplined, and often difficult training. Toward the end of Doris Dorrie's film *How to Cook Your Life* (2007), a documentary about the life and work of chef and Soto Zen priest Edward Espe Brown (b. 1945), Brown speaks of "resting in the immediate," reciting the lines above. And elsewhere, Brown describes his struggle to put that principle into practice:

> *I spent years just trying to see if I could breathe. In Buddhism over and over people say follow the breath and I've studied what is allowing the breath. You can think you're allowing the breath and it turns out you're just having it go the way you tell it to go. And then every so often you notice something about your breath like, "oh, I guess I was creating that after all." It's very hard to have experience that's really actually fresh and new, immediate. But that seems to be extremely powerful, extremely important for*

waking up in some way rather than just "can I get better at creating the experience I should be having."

As this description implies, if we are to rest in the immediate we must first relinquish the urge to control whatever we are experiencing. Like the heaving ocean, our rising and falling breath is at it is. To accept it as it is, we must first become aware of the impulse to make our breath—or any other element of our experience—conform to our expectations. But over time, Brown's experience suggests, we can learn to put our conditioning and our drive toward attainment into abeyance. Freeing ourselves from what Karen Horney called the "tyranny of the shoulds," we can rest in the freshness of our immediate experience.

In other words, we can become like Babcock's little duck, reposing in the immediate. But having learned to do so, can we also repose in "infinity"? Can we, too, become part of the heaving ocean? "He has made himself part of the boundless," writes Babcock of the little duck, "by easing himself into it just where it touches him." Babcock's assertion brings to mind a revered text of the Soto school of Zen, Shih-t'ou His-ch'ien's *Sandokai*, whose title is sometimes translated as "The Identity of the Relative and the Absolute." In this eighth-century poem, Shih-t'ou (b. 700) declares that the relative and absolute dimensions of our experience are not two but one. They fit together like a lid on a box. They meet and unite like two arrows in the air. As Roshi Pat Enkyo O'Hara explains in her talk on this text, what Shih-t'ou is telling us is that "our human nature does not obstruct our Buddha-nature." Although we may not be aware of it, we are at once historical and timeless, human and boundless, ordinary and infinite in nature. And we can touch the absolute, boundless dimension of our nature by becoming truly intimate with our messy, moment-to-moment experience, just as it is.

"The Little Duck" was published in *The New Yorker* on October 4, 1947. An expansive, free-verse poem in the manner of Robinson Jeffers, it occupies the better part of two facing pages. Babcock's general themes are impermanence and the opposition of "culture to nature." Nature takes the form of a fierce coastal storm, which has left widespread detritus and a fifty-ton, overturned rock in its wake. Human culture is epitomized by destroyed cottages "whose porches were over-ambitious, playing host to the ocean." Within this context, Babcock's little duck is seen as an imperturbable survivor, whose serene poise co-exists with the destruction all around. Edward Espe Brown recalls that his mother loved "The Little Duck," which appeared shortly before her early death.

19 September 2012

This Is, Because That Is

"Where did this bread come from?" asked a guest at our dinner table. "It's delicious." To that question, there is a very short answer. But there is also a longer answer that goes to the heart of Buddhist meditative practice.

The short answer is that the Deli-Style Rye we were enjoying came from Sisters Kneading Dough, a home bakery in Almond, New York. Every Friday afternoon, the sisters Beth and Jayne arrive at Quest Farm with their trays of bread and muffins, still warm from the oven. On that particular Friday, my wife, Robin, and I also arrived, and we came home with the Deli-Style Rye, along with a loaf of Robin's favorite, Cinnamon Swirl. That, in short, is where the bread on our table came from.

The longer answer is that the bread came from sources too numerous to mention. Deli-Style Rye is made from organic bread flour (wheat and barley), whole wheat flour, water, whole rye flour, caraway seeds, honey, yeast, and canola oil. And each of these ingredients has a history of its own. Without the work of the bees and their keepers, there would have been no honey. Without sunlight, water, earth, and the labors of the farmers, distributors, truckers, and the rest, there would have been no flour, yeast, or canola oil. Without our driving to Quest Farm on a Friday afternoon, the Deli-style Rye would never have reached our home. Like anything else that we might conventionally regard as a single thing, the bread on our table was an aggregate of countless, interconnected things, without which it could not have come into being. And as its quick disappearance demonstrated, it was not really a solid object but a transitory node in the web of life, an event in a never-ending process.

In classical Buddhist teachings, this process is known as "dependent origination." Descriptions of the process identify twelve links of causation and tend toward the esoteric, but the underlying principle can be stated in a few words:

This is, because that is.
This is not, because that is not.
This comes to be, because that comes to be.
This ceases to be, because that ceases to be.

As Zen master Thich Nhat Hanh observes, these simple sentences state the "Buddhist genesis," and the main tenets of Buddhist thought, including the doctrines of impermanence and emptiness, flow from this primary source. Beyond its philosophical import, the principle of dependent origination also helps to explain the nature of conditioned suffering. And in at least three ways, a clear understanding of this ancient principle can relieve the anxiety endemic to Western culture.

To begin with, the principle of dependent origination prompts the recognition that events have multiple causes. Whether the event in question be an unexpected rainbow or a sudden eruption of anger, events within and around us do not come out of nowhere. They arise from discernible causes and conditions. The Vipassana teacher Christina Feldman offers two vivid analogies for this process:

> *It's a little bit like a snowstorm—the coming together of a certain temperature, a certain amount of precipitation, a certain amount of wind co-creating a snow storm. Or it's like the writing of a book: one needs an idea, one needs a pen, one needs paper, one needs the ability to write. It's not necessarily true that first I must have this and then I must have this in a certain sequential order, but rather that the coming together of certain causes and conditions allows this particular phenomenon or this particular experience to be born.*

Understanding "how things come together," Feldman goes on to say, helps us to understand that what occurs in our inner and outer worlds is not "a series of aimless accidents" but the natural consequence of causes and conditions. And that understanding can alleviate the sense of being a powerless victim. By recognizing how conditions have converged to create a negative state, we can begin to see a way out. Having realized that "life is not random chaos," we can find "another way of being."

To be sure, the recognition that one's physical or emotional suffering has multiple causes can engender frustration, particularly if those causes are not self-evident. To unearth and address them might require the assistance of a therapist or health professional. But even without knowing specific causes or conditions, we can experience the second benefit of understanding dependent origination, namely the recognition that our conditioned suffering is not a permanent thing. It had a beginning, and it may well have an end. For anyone in serious physical or emotional trouble, the sentence, "This ceases to be, because that ceases to be" can be more than a succinct description of the laws of reality. It can come as a timely reassurance, if not a life-preserving revelation.

To say as much, however, is not to imply that those who are in difficulty need only wait until conditions change in their favor. For if the first benefit of understanding dependent origination is the recognition of multiple causation, and the second a renewed acknowledgement of impermanence, the third is the realization that we ourselves are links in the causal chain. Stopping to look into that chain, we can see how our present state of mind, be it anger or sorrow or elation, arose from concrete causes and conditions. We can see that our present state of mind is itself becoming a cause, creating future conditions for ourselves and others. And over time we can learn to act—or refrain from acting—in accordance with those insights.

3 October 2012

Dropping and Adding

During my years of teaching at Alfred University, I often found myself holding a piece of paper known as a Drop/Add Form. With this form in hand, students petitioned their advisors and professors to permit them to drop a burdensome course or add a desirable one or otherwise navigate the academic system. In this way students learned to make judicious choices and take responsibility for their decisions. Meanwhile, we professors learned to use a ballpoint rather than felt-tip pen when signing a multi-carboned form.

So far as I know, Drop/Add Forms are peculiar to academic life. They are not to be found in any other line of work. But the need those forms answer and the process they represent transcend the boundaries of academia. Dropping-and-adding, it might be said, is the heartbeat of everyday life, whether the item being dropped or added is tangible or intangible, conceptual or concrete. Sometimes, as in the case of mandatory retirement, the dropping of a habitual activity is not a matter of choice. Likewise, the adding of an activity or device or medication to one's daily round may be prescribed rather than freely chosen. But often the choice to drop or add may be more voluntary than one supposes, particularly if what is being dropped or added is a personal habit. And meditative awareness can play an integral role in that process, whether the habit be one of thought, feeling, speech, or behavior.

In her essay "Consciousness, Attention, and Awareness," the Zen-trained teacher Toni Packer has this to say about habits and awareness:

> *Sometimes people say, "I ought to drop this habit, but I can't." No one is asking us to drop anything. How can we drop things when we are in our customary thinking and suffering mode? We can drop a bowl of cereal, but our habitual reactions need to be seen thoroughly as they are taking place. When there is awareness, a reaction that is seen and understood to be a hindrance diminishes on its own. It may take a lot of repeated suffering, but a moment comes when the energy of seeing takes the place of the habit. That is all. Seeing is empty of self. The root of habit too is empty.*

Viewed in this way, the process of dropping habits seems as natural as swimming—once one has learned to swim. Through the cultivation of meditative awareness, our habits and habitual reactions are exposed. And once exposed, they gradually erode. The energy of habit gives way to the "energy of seeing."

In his book *The Power of Habit*, Charles Duhigg essentially concurs with Toni Packer but offers a more methodical approach. Drawing on scientific studies of habit formation, Duhigg explains that habits emerge "because the brain is constantly looking for ways to save effort." By converting routines such as walking and eating into habits, the brain conserves its energies, allowing it to focus on more advanced activities, such as "inventing spears, irrigation systems, and, eventually, airplanes and video games." In this process of conversion, a conscious choice becomes an unconscious habit. And though the process is complex, it can be reduced to a three-step pattern, known as the "habit loop":

> *This process within our brains is a three-step loop. First, there is a* cue, *a trigger that tells your brain to go into automatic mode and which habit to use. Then there is the* routine, *which can be physical or mental or emotional. Finally, there is a* reward, *which helps your brain figure out if this particular loop is worth remembering for the future.*

If the loop does endure, it becomes automatic, as cue and reward become intertwined, and a "powerful sense of anticipation and craving emerges." Out of this fusion, "a habit is born."

But can that habit be subsequently dropped? Can we replace it with another? According to the studies cited by Duhigg, our habits never really leave us. They are "encoded in the structures of our brain[s]." But with effort, a second layer of habit can be added, effectively replacing the first. As might be expected, such an effort requires motivation, determination, and self-discipline. And it also requires an awareness of "cue," "routine," and "reward," even as those steps in the process are occurring.

As an example, Duhigg cites his own habit of eating a cookie at around three o'clock every afternoon. Once he became conscious of this habit, which was adding inches to his waistline, he experimented with cue, routine, and reward, watching his responses at each stage of the process. In the manner of a Vipassana practitioner, he closely monitored his urges and became intimate with his changing thoughts and feelings.

Duhigg's experiment succeeded. The cue, he discovered, was the time of day: three to four o'clock. The routine was getting up from his desk, going to the cafeteria for his cookie, and conversing with colleagues at the cash register. And the reward, he found to his surprise, was not the satisfaction of a sugar craving but the pleasure of social contact. Having thus identified the motive driving his habit, he replaced his "routine" with a new one: chatting for ten minutes with a colleague in mid-afternoon. At the end of the workday he felt better, and in a few weeks' time, his cookie-habit disappeared.

As Duhigg acknowledges, not every habit can be so easily replaced. There is no quick fix for deep-seated habits and addictions—or Drop/Add Forms to facilitate the process. But as Duhigg's experience illustrates, and as his research amply demonstrates, it is possible to drop destructive habits and replace them with new ones. And that way freedom lies.

17 October 2012

Taking Care of Our Lives

Melody Babbitt lives on Main Street in Pueblo, Colorado, a city of 106,595 once described as the "Pittsburgh of the West" but now enduring hard times. One of several Pueblo residents profiled on the PBS program *Need to Know* (October 5, 2012), Melody is an outreach specialist for the state of Colorado. She helps disabled Americans find work. Melody earns $40,000 a year and carries health insurance, but after three required abdominal surgeries that her insurance didn't cover, she found herself deeply in debt and filed for bankruptcy. Now she needs a fourth operation and doesn't have the money. "I'm procrastinating and postponing the surgery," she tells journalist John Larson, the program's narrator, as she sweeps her front porch. "I will eventually. But I can't right now. I just can't afford it."

Melody Babbitt's plight is compelling, but no less compelling is the image we are left with: that of an American woman in her late forties, telling her story of hardship while sweeping her front porch. In the midst of financial constraints so severe that she won't allow herself to go to the movies, she is sweeping her porch. Faced with economic conditions she had no reason to expect and is virtually powerless to control, she is taking care of her home. By extension, it might be said, she is also taking care of her life.

That is an abiding purpose for most of us, I suspect, and it is also a central purpose of Zen meditation. People often come to Zen practice because their minds are unsettled and their lives are in disarray. After a few months—or even weeks—of daily practice, many find that their minds are becoming calmer and clearer, and that order is returning to their lives. And should they continue beyond that point, setting aside at least ten minutes a day for meditation, they may also find that the practice which helped them regain their balance is also helping them sustain it. For in three distinct ways, Zen practice can help us take care of our lives.

First and most evident, Zen practice encourages an attitude of caring toward one's immediate environment. Visit a Zen monastery, and you are likely to be struck by the order and cleanliness of your surroundings. That impression stems in part from the austerity of the furnishings, the careful placement of calligraphic drawings, incense bowls, and other elements of décor. But the order of the *zendo* also reflects a cardinal principle of Zen teachings, namely that everything in one's immediate environment, including inanimate objects, is worthy of respect. Further, it reflects the belief that the tasks of caretaking and housecleaning, often belittled as menial, are every bit as worthy as other, more exalted work. And, most of all, it expresses the understanding that "outer" and "inner" forms of order are parts of a whole, if not one and the same. By sweeping the floor, you are also sweeping your mind.

To be sure, one's mind may remain unswept and disordered in even the most orderly surroundings. Indeed, to someone in acute distress, the orderly ambiance of an office or waiting room may be experienced as less a consolation than an affront. But just as it is possible to care for a room or house or landscape, it is also possible to care for one's state of mind, whatever it may be. In Buddhist teachings, states of mind are known as "mental formations." Thich Nhat Hanh's tradition lists fifty-one mental formations, ranging from agitation to craving to serenity. The way to take care of them, Zen teachings advise, is, first, to remember that they are "empty"—which is to say, impermanent—and, second, to practice what Buddhism calls "mindfulness of the mind." When you are irritable, you know you are irritable. When you are calm, you know you are calm. By bringing a relaxed, non-judgmental awareness to your present state of mind, you release your attachment to it, allowing it to change of its own accord. By so doing, you catch the spark before it becomes a conflagration, the moment of sadness before it becomes a downward spiral. In this way, you take care of your mind.

Beyond the care of one's immediate environment and one's mental state, however, there is a deeper form of caring, which might be characterized as taking care of life itself. Those who have survived a life-threatening illness often report a quickened appreciation of their lives, attendant to a heightened awareness of their mortality. To engender that appreciation, not only under life-threatening circumstances but also in our daily lives, is a central aim of Zen meditation. That is why Zen monastics chant the somber imperative

"Take heed; do not squander your life" at the close of day, and why Zen teachings enjoin us to clarify the "Great Matter of Life and Death," by which is meant the impermanence of all conditioned things, including and especially our very lives. At the intellectual level, that truth is little more than a banality. But having truly felt it at the emotional and indeed the visceral levels, we are less likely to squander our lives in pursuit of petty satisfactions and distracting entertainments. And having sharpened our awareness of the preciousness of our lives, we may come to value, appreciate, and take care of them, whatever afflictions and hardships come our way.

That is a lofty goal, of course, and few of us are up to it every day. But the effort to attain it can start with a straightening of the spine, a few conscious breaths—and the careful sweeping of one's front porch.

31 October 2012

Realizing

One evening last week, as I was reading Khaled Hosseini's novel *The Kite Runner*, I paused at the end of a paragraph. That paragraph, I realized, had just given me exceptional pleasure. An aesthetic pleasure, to be sure, but no less keen for that.

Here is the paragraph, which depicts a winter morning in Kabul:

> *Here is what I do on the first day of snowfall every year: I step out of the house early in the morning, still in my pajamas, hugging my arms against the chill. I find the driveway, my father's car, the walls, the trees, the rooftops, and the hills buried under a foot of snow. I smile. The sky is seamless and blue, the snow so white my eyes burn. I shovel a handful of the fresh snow into my mouth, listen to the muffled stillness broken only by the cawing of crows. I walk down the front steps, barefoot, and call for Hassan to come out and see.*

There are many reasons why a reader might relish this paragraph. My own enjoyment stemmed, in a general way, from the clarity, directness, and freshness of Hosseini's prose. More specifically, it derived from Hosseini's sensuous, evocative imagery, his deft handling of cadence, and his construction of an intimate narrative voice: that of a grown man tenderly recalling his childhood. Experiencing all those qualities and more, I experienced the complex pleasure they provided.

Yet, had I not paused, I might never have realized what I was experiencing. Almost certainly, I was thinking as I read, but thinking is not the same as realizing the experience one is having, an experience that includes but is not limited to thought. Understandably, much of our educational effort focuses on teaching students how to think, critically and conceptually. Far more rare, however, is systematic training in how to *realize* what one is experiencing. And toward that end, meditative practice can play an important, complementary role, not only in education but also in our everyday lives.

In speaking of realization, I am not referring to what James Joyce rather grandly called an epiphany: a kind of revelation, often experienced in the most mundane surroundings. Nor am I speaking of what Robert Frost called a "clarification of life": that "momentary stay against confusion" which good poems, often in their closing lines, can engender. Rather, I am speaking of what the American historian Drew Gilpin Faust, in her book *This Republic of Suffering*, describes as the act of "realizing." Events occur, whether we want them to or not. To realize those events, Faust asserts, is "to render [them] real" in our own minds. In the language of Zen, it is to make occurrences within and around us present to our awareness.

There are manifold ways to accomplish that purpose, but for the Zen practitioner the central way is the practice of *zazen*, or seated meditation. In practicing the form of zazen known as *shikantaza*, or "just sitting," one sits without an agenda, object, or method, other than to assume an upright, relaxed posture, settle into stillness, and become present for whatever is going on. Breathing in, we know we are breathing in; breathing out, we know we are breathing out. If we are experiencing elation, we are aware of it; if we are experiencing craving, sorrow, or anger, we acknowledge those passing emotions as well. Maintaining the relaxed, aligned, and resilient posture of zazen, we may find that our balanced posture itself is helping us remain open to whatever comes. For, as Shunryu Suzuki Roshi once observed, the posture of zazen allows us to accept the disagreeable with the agreeable. It allows us to realize what is there.

That is difficult to do under the best of circumstances, but it is especially challenging if the reality we are experiencing runs counter to our preconceptions, prejudices, or deeply held beliefs. In *This Republic of Suffering*, Drew Gilpin Faust provides dramatic examples of that challenge, as she examines the tension between the Victorian belief in the "Good Death" and the horrific realities of the American Civil War. Prior to 1861, she explains, the "prevailing Christian narrative" portrayed the believer dying a natural death at home, surrounded by family and leaving this world in a state of peaceful acceptance. But the realities of the Civil War were otherwise. Men died in unprecedented numbers—7,863 were killed at Gettysburg alone—and often in states other than peaceful acceptance. Beyond that, the fact that so many died and were buried far from home, often unidentified, deprived their survivors of a concrete, necessary certainty. In the absence of irrefutable physical evidence, it became difficult, if not impossible, for loved ones to realize their loss, accept it, and move on. In one poignant instance described by Faust, a grieving widow requested that her husband's remains be exhumed from their faraway grave. Only then could she fully realize the loss she had incurred. Only then could she begin the process of mourning.

Fortunately, the stakes are seldom so high in everyday life, but the choice remains much the same. Whether we are reading a novel set in Kabul or witnessing, at a distance, the latest atrocity in Syria's own civil war, we can content ourselves with thinking and having opinions about our experience, enlisting the abstractions of language for that purpose. Or, with the help of meditative awareness, we can endeavor to *realize* our experience, fully and concretely. And much depends on the difference.

14 November 2012

The Handwritten Word

During the last few days of October, when Hurricane Sandy was threatening Western New York, state and local officials advised us as to the important documents we should take with us in the event of an evacuation: deeds, home-insurance policies, birth certificates, passports, and the like. In preparation, we should assemble those documents and place them in a waterproof envelope.

Sound advice, to be sure. But as I read that official list, I thought of a less than official item I would add to it: the file of documents I have kept for years under my father's well-worn Bible. Contained in that file are notes, letters, and cards from friends and family, including letters from my deceased mother; birthday cards from my wife; holiday cards from my daughter-in-law; and a variety of notes from my son, some of them dating from his early childhood. Unlike the policies and passports, those documents are irreplaceable. And all were written by hand, which makes them all the more valuable.

That value, I might point out, is more than sentimental. It is historical and spiritual. The novelist Philip Hensher, author of *The Missing Ink* (Macmillan, 2012), has argued, with ample corroboration, that "we are at a moment when handwriting seems to be about to vanish from our lives," having been supplanted by the printed—and now the digital—word. If Hensher is right, we would do well to cherish whatever handwritten documents remain extant, irrespective of their author or content. But even if we believe that handwriting, having survived for 5000 years, will always be with us, the act of writing by hand is worthy of renewed attention, if not of veneration. For in the handwritten word, it might be said, the authentic human self is concretely embodied. And the handwritten note or letter, however rough or polished, affords a depth of intimacy between writer and reader that print can only approximate. Little wonder that the world's great spiritual traditions, Zen included, have accorded the handwritten word—or character—a place of honor, whether the handwritten text be the Torah, the Quran, the Heart Sutra, or the Book of Kells.

Yet, if the Zen tradition shares a common regard for the handwritten text, it differs in one important respect. In contrast to such treasures as the Lindisfarne Gospels, which were slowly and meticulously transcribed by medieval monks, some of the most revered texts of the classical Zen tradition are in essence improvisations. Executed spontaneously, without revision, they reflect the state of the practitioner's mind at the moment of composition. In a frame on our wall, my wife and I have one such text: a rendition of the Zen slogan "This is It," inscribed in a fluent English script by the Venerable Thich Nhat Hanh. Stamped in red ink with Thich Nhat

Hanh's personal "chop," this inscription is not a reproduction. On the contrary, it is an original work of calligraphic art, and to contemplate it for any length of time is to feel the presence of a true Zen master, whose clear and spacious mind, at the moment of inscription, is unmistakably reflected in the words he inscribed.

By the same token, Thich Nhat Hanh's inscription also affords access to its author's unguarded heart. I am reminded of Sylvia Townsend Warner's comment, apropos of the great letter-writers of the past. *Look, they say. These black signs on white paper, they are me. My blood ran with this ink.* And I am reminded, even more, of my own encounters over the years with the handwritten words of writers living and dead, among them W. B. Yeats, Gerard Manley Hopkins, Loren Eiseley, Adrienne Rich, and Seamus Heaney. In every case the connection thus established transcended the merely literary.

As I reflect this morning on those encounters, one in particular stands out. During a visit to Dublin in the 1980s, I stopped in at the National Library of Ireland, where I was given permission to view and indeed to hold the original manuscript of Patrick Kavanagh's "The Great Hunger" (1942), one of the seminal poems of modern Irish writing. As I examined the manuscript under a green-shaded library lamp, Kavanagh's poem became more than a literary monument. Scrawled in the pages of a college blue book, it became an avenue to its author, whose vulnerabilities as well as gifts were on full display. "I wasn't really a writer," Kavanagh once remarked. "I had seen a strange beautiful light on the hills and that was all." In Kavanagh's roughhewn but expressive hand, both the erstwhile Monaghan farmer and the gifted lyric poet were vividly present. To encounter both at such close proximity was as moving as it was illuminating.

The manuscript of "The Great Hunger" is safely archived in the National Library, and the poem itself is firmly established in the canon of Irish verse. Yet the blue book I was holding was no more permanent than its dry, acid-bearing pages. And from the vantage point of Zen teachings, neither was the self reflected in Kavanagh's script. Rather, it was the provisional self of the poet Patrick Kavanagh, compacted of his temperament, his literary and social culture, his historical moment, and other, contingent elements too numerous to mention. In her book *Nothing Special* the Zen teacher Charlotte Joko Beck likens the self to a whirlpool in a stream, subject to continuous change and eventual dispersal. All the more reason to conserve the handwritten documents in our possession, which provide a trace of that temporary self, whether their authors be Zen masters, celebrated writers, or members of our families. And all the more reason to pick up a pen.

28 November 2012

Wise Attention

According to a recent report on the NBC Nightly News, American police have been running stop signs and causing serious accidents, so distracted have they become by the computers in their cars. To address the problem, the Fort Wayne, Indiana police department has installed devices that freeze the computer's keys whenever the patrol car's speed exceeds fifteen miles per hour.

This situation may be uniquely ironic, but the underlying problem is hardly peculiar to the police. On the contrary, in the age of the Internet and ubiquitous mobile devices, distraction has become endemic. With so many objects summoning our attention, where shall we direct it? On what objects should we place our minds?

In many situations, such as when operating a chainsaw, we have little choice but to attend to the task at hand. Our safety depends upon it. But in many others, we do have a choice, and should we elect to engage in meditation, Buddhist teachings offer a variety of objects on which we might place our minds. If you are already practicing meditation, you know that the most basic object is the breath—its comings and goings, its length and texture. But beyond that, the Teachings of the Elders, as they are called, prescribe four general objects (or "foundations") of mindful awareness.

According to the *Four Foundations of Mindfulness* (*Satipatthana Sutra*), a fundamental text of the Theravadan school, those objects are the body (its posture, movements, and parts); the feelings (pleasant, unpleasant, neutral); transitory mental states; and "objects of mind." The last of these foundations includes such objects as the "Five Hindrances" (craving, aversion, sloth, agitation, and doubt), which impede meditation, and the "Seven Factors of Enlightenment," which are to be cultivated through systematic attention. By contemplating the hindrances, we gradually diminish their power. And by placing our attention on the Factors of Enlightenment, which include concentration, tranquility, and equanimity, we purify our minds, freeing them of "mental afflictions."

Zen Buddhism is a late flowering of the classical tradition, and though its teachings incorporate elements of Theravadan practice, its prescribed objects of mindfulness are fewer in number and less introspective in character. Broadly speaking, the Zen practitioner is enjoined to focus on the breath, whether by counting out-breaths (*susokkan*) or "following" the breath (*zuisokukan*); on koans such as "What is this?" or "What is the sound of one hand?"; and on one's sitting presence itself (*shikantaza*). By so doing, the Zen disciple endeavors to cut through conceptual thought with the "sword of attention," to extinguish the ego's promiscuous delusions, and to abide continuously in the present moment—the "only moment," as Zen master Thich Nhat Hanh often puts it, "where life is available to us."

All of Zen's traditional objects are worthy of attention, but lest the practice become narrow and rigid, it is important to remain open to other possibilities. The Vipassana teacher Jack Kornfield, who speaks of meditation as an art, warns against fixating on any one object or method of paying attention. Instead he advocates a flexible approach, in which the practitioner's "wise attention" becomes a "zoom lens," opening from a concentrated close-up to the middle distance to a panoramic view, depending on present conditions. Practicing "close-up" attention, we focus intently on a sensation, feeling, or thought, eventually becoming absorbed in the object of attention. Practicing in the middle distance, we witness whatever is occurring, be it a mental event or an occurrence in our immediate surroundings. And practicing panoramic attention, we open the mind's lens to its widest angle, allowing our awareness to become "like space or the sky." In this unconditioned awareness, thoughts, images, feelings, and sounds come and go, as though they were clouds in the sky. And as a final step, we can focus on awareness itself, observing its "clear, transparent, [and] timeless" nature. Like open space itself, unconditioned awareness allows all things, without being limited by any one of them.

Jack Kornfield also recommends the practice of listening to the "sounds of the universe," which is to say, the sounds in our immediate environment. This practice, Kornfield notes, "brings the mind to a naturally balanced state of openness and attention." In similar fashion, the Theravadan teacher Ajahn Amaro encourages us to meditate on the "inner sound," or the "sound of silence." In this esoteric practice, known as *nada yoga*, we listen first to the sounds around us, whatever they may be. Within that body of ambient sound, we may detect a "continuous, high-pitched inner sound." By concentrating on this "nada" sound, we cultivate stability of mind, even as we heighten our awareness of the insubstantiality of thoughts, feelings, and states of mind. And if we persist in the practice, Amaro observes, we may come to realize the "orderly perfection in which the world is balanced within the heart of vibrant silence."

To place the mind on the "nada" sound, or indeed upon any of the traditional objects of Buddhist meditation, is a far cry from placing it on the latest garish pop-up on our computer screens. Yet in this instance the issue of "high" versus "low," or "wholesome" versus "unwholesome" objects of attention, is somewhat beside the point. For those of us who spend hours online, claims on our attention are countless and more or less continuous. Given such conditions, it behooves us to remember that where the disposition of attention is concerned, we have a choice, and that our power to choose can be strengthened by daily practice. Moment by moment, it might be said, we are creating the reality we inhabit. And to an extent that may surprise us, that reality is determined by where and how we have placed our minds.

12 December 2012

Snow

Dr. Friederike Boissevain is a German oncologist and seasoned Zen practitioner. By her own admission, her meditative practice is imperfect—or "crooked," as she describes it. Rather than remain focused and fully aware of the present moment, she finds herself wandering off into the "land of dreams and worries." But, crooked though it be, her practice has supported her daily work with the sick and the dying. "The most important thing I ever did," she reflects, "was to sit down once." That act set "something in motion that cannot be stopped. This is not because of trust in something but because of experience . . . The snow of dharma covers everything, whether we see it or not."

The snow of dharma? In Buddhist teachings the word dharma has three distinct meanings. In its simplest usage, the word refers to phenomena: the things of this world. "Aware of the impermanence of all dharmas," the practitioner silently recites, "I breathe in. / Contemplating the impermanence of all dharmas, I breathe out." But the word dharma can also refer to the body of Buddhist teachings, as in the Zen chant "Opening this Dharma," where those teachings are described as "incomparably profound and minutely subtle." And last, *dharma* can refer to the "laws of reality," most prominently those of impermanence, no-self, "dependent origination," and the interconnectedness of all conditioned things. As one master put it, if we can sit still and *know* we are sitting still, the laws of reality will be revealed to us.

Of those many laws, the inescapable law of impermanence is the most easily verified by direct experience. If you wish to verify it for yourself, may I suggest that you sit still, in a stable, upright posture, and pay attention to what is occurring within and around you. If you wish, you may close your eyes, as Vipassana practitioners do. Or you may leave them half-open and focused on a point three feet in front of you, as Zen teachings prescribe.

If you choose to close your eyes, you can readily observe that within your body and your inner life, nothing is permanent or solid. A moment ago, your in-breath was present; now it is absent. At the start of your sitting, your breathing was fast and shallow; now it is deep and slow. Before, your lower back felt strained; now, as you bring awareness to your spine and your lumbar region, the sensations of pain begin to subside. When you first sat down, you were feeling tense or sad or elated, but as you train your awareness on your state of mind, you realize that in the time you've been sitting, your mood has changed. Indeed, everything appears to be in flux—everything but your awareness of the changes.

Should you elect to keep your eyes open, you can also verify the law of impermanence, merely by observing your immediate surroundings. On Sunday evenings, especially in the summer, those who attend the sessions of the Falling Leaf Sangha, our local Zen practice group, witness the gradual and sometimes beguiling changes in the light around us. We meet in a spacious, high-ceilinged room, whose tall windows look out on rolling hills. During the course of an hour, the light streaming through the windows brightens, dims, and eventually disappears. Experiencing those changes, moment by moment, from the vantage point of a still and silent awareness, we understand impermanence not as a concept or Zen tenet but as an experiential fact, as palpably real as the darkness gathering around us.

To be sure, it is easier to acknowledge the fact of fading light than to witness, as Dr. Boissevain does in her daily work, the impermanence of a human life ebbing and coming to an end. But by gaining, through meditative practice, what Thich Nhat Hanh calls "the insight of impermanence," and by deepening that insight through years of diligent practice, we can cultivate the strength and courage to meet even the most troubling forms of impermanence, namely our own and that of our loved ones, with a balanced and compassionate mind.

Models of courageous realism abound in the literature of Zen, and nowhere more than in the writings of the Japanese poet Matsuo Basho (1644-1694), a Zen practitioner who transformed the haiku from a pastime into a vehicle for serious poetry. In one of his most celebrated haiku ("Summer grasses: / all that remains of great soldiers' / imperial dreams"), as in his travels throughout Japan, Basho contemplated the impermanence of life. And in a poetic sequence entitled "While Reading Basho," the American poet Hayden Carruth (1921-2008), writing across four centuries, recognizes his affinity with the earlier poet:

The snow falls. Bashō,
    we are very far apart,
        and snow is falling.

I'm almost eighty,
    and as I watch the meadow's
        brown grass vanishing

beneath this whiteness
    how can I not share with you
        the poignancy of

passing time?

In this quiet lyric, Carruth pays homage to Basho by adopting his signature form. Each of Carruth's stanzas is a haiku, with a syllabic pattern of 5-7-5. Beyond this formal connection, however, a deeper solidarity may be discerned in Carruth's recognition of impermanence, embodied here in vanishing brown grass and falling snow. "Why / is it so hard," Carruth inquires elsewhere, "to get rid of time?" "Is it because so soon I am going to die?"

    Hayden Carruth was not a Zen practitioner, but he was drawn to Asian poetry and culture, and in his lines for Basho he demonstrates an intuitive understanding of the workings of the dharma. To avail ourselves of its support, his lines suggest, we have only to quiet our minds and fully acknowledge the reality of change. We have only to let it snow.

26 December 2012

Unwelcome Sounds

As I sit at my desk this morning, I am listening unwillingly to the rhythmic, reverberant, and unrelenting blows of a pile driver on cold steel. *Wham*! (Pause). *Wham*! (Pause). *Wham*! The crashes continue for another twenty minutes, as they have for the past few weeks. Charitably regarded, this disturbance of the peace represents the embodied spirit of Progress. Alfred University is building a new recreation center, a half block away from our home. But for many of us who live or work nearby, the noise has been the aural equivalent of a chronic, throbbing toothache. It has been an unwelcome sound.

In this it is far from alone. Most of us, I suspect, have our lists of unwelcome sounds, and more often than not, those sounds are beyond our power to abate, much less eliminate. Under such conditions, a scriptural reminder might be helpful: "And we exhort you, brethren . . . be patient with them all" (*1 Thessalonians* 5:14). But help may also be found in Buddhist teachings, which offer three distinct practices for dealing with unwanted feelings and sensations.

Include everything

To be human is to have preferences. Sweet over sour. Consonant over dissonant. Quiet over loud. And to enforce our preferences, we include certain things in our awareness and exclude others. But as Zen teacher Roshi Pat Enkyo O'Hara explains, it is possible to do otherwise:

> *Just imagine what it would be like if you were to include everything that arises. Usually, all of us only include a certain amount: what we like, what we are willing to see about ourselves and others. We don't include the things we don't like about ourselves or about conditions and situations. We push them away. Denial.*

As a countermeasure, O'Hara exhorts us "to constantly include everything that is arising." As an example, she recalls her experience in a soup kitchen, where she became consciously aware of her disgust ("Is this man going to throw up on me?"). By so doing, she opened herself to "reality, to the conditions of the world of which we are a part."

The phrase "include everything" gives O'Hara's practice a fresh turn, but the attitude she advocates is rooted in the *Faith-Mind Sutra*, a classic Zen text. The putative author is Seng-ts'an, the Third Zen Patriarch, who reassures us that "the Great Way is not difficult / for those not attached to preferences." To "set up what you like against what you dislike / is the disease of the mind." To heal ourselves, we must put our likes and dislikes in abeyance, allowing things to exist as they are.

Undertaken intelligently, the practice of inclusion can conduce to greater openness, tolerance, and compassion. In my experience, however, the practice requires vigilant self-awareness, lest the effort to be inclusive foster self-deception. Encountering an unpleasant sound, sight, or feeling, I may think that I am including that sensation or feeling in my awareness. But I may also be fooling myself.

Investigate experience

If we can truly accept an unpleasant reality, that practice alone can pacify our minds. But should that effort fall short, we can take the further step of investigating our experience, with a view to gaining insight as well as immediate relief. This practice may be divided into two stages, the first pertaining to external reality, the second to the practitioner's internal response.

One summer many years ago, I found myself subjected to disconcerting sound. At the time I was living in a room at Trinity College, Dublin. My window looked out on Pearse Street, a noisy thoroughfare. The din of traffic was constant—or so I thought, until I stopped to listen. Sitting in zazen one evening, I turned my attention from my annoyance to the sound itself, and I was surprised to find that it was neither constant nor in itself unpleasant. Listening closely, I noticed that the sound came in waves, as traffic halted at the stop light, fell silent, and resumed a minute later. Experienced in this way, the once-troubling sound became an object of curiosity rather than consternation, and my tension eased.

In that same sitting, I also examined my emotional response. If the sound itself was not unpleasant, what had caused the inner conflict? What beliefs, assumptions, or unacknowledged expectations had created my internal tension, and with it my negative perceptions? Those questions could scarcely be answered—or laid to rest—in a single sitting. But merely by entertaining them, I released myself from the confines I'd created.

Practice non-duality

In the *Faith-Mind Sutra*, Seng-Ts'an offers further advice. "In this world 'as it really is,'" he writes, "there is neither self nor other-than-self. / / To know this Reality directly / is possible only through practicing non-duality. / When you live this non-separation, / all things manifest the One, and nothing is excluded."

In our ordinary experience there is indeed a "self" and "other." And much of the time, that imagined separate self is at odds with a perceived other, whether it be a person of a different class, nation, or persuasion or the world itself, where inclement weather alters our plans and pile drivers intrude upon our peace. But as Seng-Ts'an observes, in undifferentiated reality there is no self or other, no Hearer or Heard. And as the Indian sage Tilopa reminds us, with practice it is possible to "remain in the flow of sheer awareness," where "the appearance of division and conflict / disappears into original reality." Dwelling in that awareness, we can experience the world not as concatenation of solid things but as an unending flow, where nothing is excluded, and even the *wham*-pause-*wham* of a pile driver is heard as the pulse of life itself.

6 February 2013

Past and Present

"He gave the art a good name," remarked the Nobel laureate Seamus Heaney of the Irish poet Dennis O'Driscoll, who died suddenly on Christmas Eve at the age of fifty-eight. Dennis was the author of nine collections of graceful, civilized verse and one of the most respected voices in contemporary Irish letters. I am saddened by his early death, as are many of his fellow writers, Irish and American, who remember him as a true gentleman and a generous friend.

I first met Dennis at the Irish Writers' Centre in Dublin in the mid-nineties. We struck up a long conversation, which grew over time into a warm, collegial friendship. Whenever I was in Dublin I would ring him up, and we would meet for lunch at O'Neill's, a Victorian pub with an excellent carvery. I brought news of American poetry. Dennis brought wit, a playful spirit, and a keen awareness of the Irish literary scene. The Irish novelist Belinda McKeon has described Dennis as a "walking encyclopedia of poetry," and that he was, but unlike many encyclopedias he was never ponderous or dull. And unlike most modern poets, he had little to do with academia. Trained in the law, he had worked in the Irish civil service since he was sixteen. In our last conversation, in June, 2009, he casually remarked that I had "all the qualities of a good lawyer." Considering its source, I took that as a compliment.

Dennis was known as a poet of the present tense. Acutely aware of the manners and mores of affluent, 21st-century Dublin, he portrayed and sometimes pinioned the culture of "fast-moving, computer-clock-watching, speed-dating / Ireland." But like many Dubliners of his generation, he was not a native of the city. He hailed from the town of Thurles (pop. 8000) in Co. Tipperary. And in his poem "Bread and Butter," he recalls the fare of a bygone time:

> *Irish taste buds configured in the bread-and-butter*
> *era, the donkey-cart-to-creamery age that no longer*
> *dares to speak its shabby name, shamefully hunger*
> *sometimes for the old values of the ham sandwich*
> *in a scruffy lunch-hour pub: fat-framed meat in oval*
> *slices, pink folds arrayed on greaseproof paper,*
> *ready, at the half-twelve rush, to be sandwiched with*
> *a wedge of processed cheddar, a slobbery tomato ring*
> *lobbed in for good measure, a tattered lettuce leaf*
> *revived under a cold water tap; white-sliced pan*
> *of pre-focaccia, pre-tortilla days, buttered up incautiously*
> *by the wheezing, plum-faced, sleeve-rolled barman;*
> *cracked plate slapped down—take it or leave it—*
> *on a sudsy Guinness beermat.*

Recalling this humble but savory lunch, the narrator finds himself remembering "a Tipperary meadow, cows / flinching from insects, fly-whisk tails / patrolling dung-encrusted hindquarters." That image prompts him to recall the "moulded cups / of mushrooms" presenting themselves at his feet.

As the narrator readily admits, he is being nostalgic. He is a long, long way from Tipperary, and his remembered images bear the patina of fond recollection. But unlike the soft nostalgia for which we of a certain age are notorious, the tone of Dennis's recollections is as objective as his images are precise. Evocative though it is of a vanished era, his poem is set in the present. And though its narrator may go on about ham sandwiches and sudsy beer mats, he never forgets where he is presently living. To be sure, his reference to such fashionable imports as focaccias may be faintly disapproving, but he does not denigrate the present or place the "old values of the ham sandwich" above the values represented, elsewhere in his poem, by a healthful regimen of "frosty fruits / smoothie, organic Caesar salad wrap, plastic tub / of watercolour melon chunks, detox glass of wheatgrass." Rather, he views the two contrasting eras with a balanced eye, as might a seasoned judge or professional historian. Neither era is superior. Neither is to be prized above the other.

To see the past in this balanced way was one of Dennis's gifts, and it is also one of the aims of Zen meditation. Zen teachings exhort us to live in the present, but that injunction should not be construed narrowly to mean excluding the past. As the essayist Chris Arthur notes, "To conceive of 'now' merely as some kind of perpetually isolated instance, shorn of all its interrelationship with other moments, seems more impoverishment than insight—an invitation to superficiality rather than to genuine engagement with the texture of the present." And in his commentary on the *Bhaddekaratta*

Sutra, Thich Nhat Hanh admonishes us to admit the past into our awareness of the present moment:

> *The present contains the past. When we understand how our internal formations cause conflicts in us, we can see how the past is in the present moment, and we will no longer be overwhelmed by the past. When the Buddha said "Do not pursue the past," he was telling us not to be overwhelmed by the past. He did not mean that we should stop looking at the past in order to observe it deeply. When we review the past and observe it deeply, if we are standing firmly in the present, we are not overwhelmed by it.*

Rereading Thich Nhat Hanh's admonition in the aftermath of Dennis's passing, I am aware of the all-too-human urge to "pursue the past." I have little doubt that the next time I visit Dublin and stop in for lunch at O'Neill's, I will miss my friend's hospitable company, his cultivated voice and gentlemanly demeanor. But I am also mindful of the need to stand "firmly in the present," and I am newly grateful for Dennis's enduring poems, which so skillfully integrate the present and the past.

20 February 2013

Cooked Carrots

Being retired now, I cook most of the meals in our home. And of late I have become a connoisseur of my wife's responses, spoken and unspoken, to what I put on our table.

Let us say that tonight's menu is Rotini with Lemon-Asparagus Sauce, a side of cooked carrots, and a Martha's Vineyard salad. After a few bites, Robin may comment on what she has just eaten, or she may not. If she is silent for very long, I begin to get curious. "How do you like it?" I venture to inquire.

"It's good," she reassures me. But her real meaning, I've come to realize, resides in her inflection. If the sauce is dry or a bit salty, "good" will take on a rising, tentative intonation, as if another verbal shoe were about to drop. If the sauce is indeed good, as opposed to bad, the word will have an affirmative but faintly impatient tone, as if to say, "Why wouldn't it be?" But if, as occasionally happens, I have outdone myself, "good" will be accompanied or replaced by "delicious," "scrumptious," or even *"bellisimo!"* At that point I will surmise that all is well, though in her own words Robin has "never been partial to cooked carrots," and at the end of the meal, a discreet pile of those little orange offenders remains on her plate.

For better or worse, I am myself partial to cooked carrots and could eat them every other night. (To which Robin might add, "and we do"). Unlike Robin, who hails from Brooklyn, I grew up in the American heartland—eastern Iowa, to be exact. And a staple of our Sunday dinners was a portion of soft, cooked carrots, bathed in the juices of thoroughly cooked roast beef. As a grade-school child I grew my own carrots in my parents' backyard garden, and I fondly remember sinking my father's garden fork into the moist black loam of eastern Iowa. Even now, as I chop carrots into quarter-inch rounds or reduce them to matchsticks for Pasta Primavera, I recall their role in our family dinners and their place in my earliest experience.

Much of that experience is foreign to Robin, as much of hers is to me. And so are the vernaculars in which we, as children and young adults, were deeply immersed. Such delectable words as *tschotske* (pron. CHOCH-kah, meaning "curio," decorative object), *schmata* (rag; inferior piece of clothing), *bubala* (a term of endearment, sometimes applied to spouses), *meshugana* (crazy, a crazy person; also applied to spouses), and *oy, gevalt!* (good grief!), all of which Robin might utter in the course of a day, were never heard in my family home—or for that matter in the entire State of Iowa. Long ago I abandoned any attempt to employ such words in conversation, lest I make myself a laughingstock. To speak Yiddish properly, not to mention expressively, requires a range of inflections and a repertoire of gestures well beyond the range of a plain-spoken, reticent Midwesterner.

Such differences of upbringing, taste, language, and temperament are of course the stuff of marriage, and if conjugal harmony is one's goal, it is essential to recognize, respect, and if possible understand them. And toward that end, Zen meditation can help.

Zen is often thought of as a solitary endeavor, and in several, obvious ways it is, but Zen meditation can also support harmonious interaction with other people, especially those with whom we live. One of my fellow practitioners, who has been married for thirty years, notes that belonging to a practice group gets him out of the house one night a week, which is probably good for his marriage. More seriously, as the Venerable Thich Nhat Hanh has often observed, the practice of mindfulness trains us to be wholly present, not only for ourselves but also for our spouses, children, and other members of our families. At its most effective, meditative practice fosters one-pointed listening and a moment-by-moment awareness of how the other person, be it wife or son or daughter, is responding to what we say or do. And over time, such awareness can transform us into better—or at least less annoying—spouses, partners, and parents, who at long last understand what to say and not to say, and when it is best to say nothing. Perhaps with luck and continuing effort, the practice of Zen may also turn a garden-variety cook into a passable family chef, who knows more often than not what his wife desires.

6 March 2013

Elsewhere

If you have a good memory for movies, you may remember *Nobody's Fool* (1994). Set in a declining town in upstate New York and based loosely on Richard Russo's comedic novel, *Nobody's Fool* stars Paul Newman as Donald "Sully" Sullivan, a feckless, sixty-year-old handyman who, in Russo's words, has "led a life of studied unpreparedness." Although he is blessed with humane instincts and a generous heart, Sully's devil-may-care attitude and his boyish penchant for mischief have too often sabotaged his better nature.

Sully's sidekick and fellow bungler of odd jobs is a garbage collector named Rub Squeers, who plays a role in Sully's adventures comparable to that of Sancho Panza in Don Quixote's. Rub is just over five feet tall. His large head sits "like a medicine ball precariously balanced on his thick shoulders." For most of his life Rub has seldom paid attention to much of anything. He finds attentiveness "hateful and exhausting," and he considers inattention "normal human behavior."

What Rub does do is *wish*, habitually and frequently. During a lull, when he and Sully are out of work, Rub wishes that "we'd just start up again like before." Later, when they do find work, Rub wishes "we were all through with this job and sitting in The Horse eating a big ole cheeseburger." Wherever Rub might be, he wishes he were elsewhere.

Rub Squeers is a fictional character, but he bears a strong resemblance to an actual person, namely Richard Russo's troubled mother. In his recent memoir *Elsewhere*, Russo remembers his mother, Jean, as an intelligent and stylish but profoundly dissatisfied woman, "lost in some labyrinth of her own thoughts and impulses." Middle-aged, divorced, and caught in an "economic cage," Jean eked out a meager living in the upstate town of Gloversville, New York, which she regarded as an "awful, awful place." When her son was admitted to the University of Arizona, Jean saw an opportunity to escape her bleak environs, and against her aging parents' wishes she went with him. Relocating in Phoenix, she began to put down roots, but after a few years she came to regard Phoenix, too, as an awful, awful place. And when her brief second marriage ended, she returned to Gloversville—only to return to Arizona a short while later. For the next two decades Jean followed her nomadic son and his family from one teaching job to another, winding up at last in Maine. But no matter where she lived, she remained unsettled, wanting always to be elsewhere.

Jean's case was no doubt extreme. In Russo's mature opinion, his mother's chronic disquiet stemmed from both her straitened economic circumstances and her mental disorder, specifically her debilitating, untreated OCD. But as a recent Harvard study has shown, Jean's habitual state of mind, however extreme, was not all that unusual. Most of us, it would seem, spend much of our lives dreaming we were elsewhere.

In their 2010 study of more than 2,200 people from ages 18 to 88, Harvard researchers Matthew Killingsworth and Daniel Gilbert found that about 47 percent of their subjects' waking hours were spent being somewhere other than in the present moment. And they also found a positive correlation between reported unhappiness and the habit of mental wandering. People are happiest, they concluded, when living in the present and focusing on their present activities.

Zen meditation can help us do just that. It can return us, time and again, to the present moment, until the habit of being present replaces the habit of being elsewhere. But lest the practice be misunderstood, it should be noted that the immediate aim of Zen is not to eradicate all wishes or abolish all desires. Rather, it is to cultivate a direct, continuous awareness of our present experience, including our wishes, daydreams, and beguiling divagations.

Rub Squeers may well be right: inattention is normal human behavior. And as Russo's memoir vividly illustrates, by ignoring the present moment and habitually engaging in wishful thinking, we can wreak merciless havoc upon ourselves and others. To become consciously aware of our wandering minds is to allow ourselves, at any given moment, a liberating choice. We can wish for and dream of another life, as it is sometimes fruitful to do. Or, conversely, we can reenter, with curiosity and wholehearted commitment, the imperfect life we are already living.

20 March 2013

Notes

Ordinary Mind

1 **"Shoveling Snow with Buddha"**: Billy Collins, *Sailing Alone Around the Room: New and Selected Poems* (Random House, 2001), 103-104.

Near and Far

5 **"Does Football Have a Future?"**: *The New Yorker*, January 31, 2011, 41-51.

6 **more likely to hear speculation**: Frank Rich, "Wallflowers at the Revolution," *New York Times*, Sunday, February 5, 2011.

The Harp of Myanmar

9 **After years of meditation**: Joshua Hammer, "A Free Woman," *The New Yorker*, January 24, 2011, 24-30.

Michio Takeyama, *Harp of Burma*, tr. Howard Hibbett (Tuttle, 1966). Kon Ichikawa's acclaimed film *The Burmese Harp* (1956) is based on Takeyama's novel.

Rest-Stroke, Free-Stroke

17 **The song of the piano**: Eugenio d' Ors, "La Cancion de la Guitarra." (*La cancion del piano es un discurso. / La cancion del cello es una elegia. / La cancion de la guitarra—es una cancion*).

Flappers

21 **The Flapper is likewise**: Jonathan Swift, *The Writings of Jonathan Swift*, ed. Robert A. Greenberg and William B. Piper (Norton, 1973), 133. In eighteenth-century British usage, a kennel is a gutter.

23 **As exercises in both**: Thich Nhat Hanh, *Present Moment, Wonderful Moment: Mindfulness Verses for Daily Living* (Parallax Press, 1990).

Reb Anderson, *Being Upright: Zen Meditation and the Bodhisattva Precepts* (Rodmell Press, 2000), 69.

One Thing at a Time

26 **In this practice**: Reb Anderson, *Being Upright: Zen Meditation and the Bodhisattva Precepts* (Rodmell Press, 2000), 70.

can serve as a fresh: Toni Packer, "Consciousness, Attention, and Awareness," in *The Wonder of Presence* (Shambhala, 2002), 136-7.

27 **settle down peacefully**: Shohaku Okumura, *Realizing Genjokoan* (Wisdom, 2010), Kindle Edition, 1260.

Gardens of Fear and Desire

29 **mental cultivation**: In Theravadan Buddhism the Pali word *bhavana*, which means "mental cultivation," is often translated as "meditation." The practice of bhavana is sometimes contrasted with that of *dhyana*, or concentrated awareness of interdependent reality. The Japanese word Zen derives from *dhyana*.

Andres Dubus III, *Townie: A Memoir* (Norton, 2011).

Just Say "Oops!"

35 T.P. Kasulis, *Zen Action, Zen Person* (University of Hawaii Press, 1981), 56-60; 101.

Grant Wilke: No stranger to Asian disciplines, Grant Wilke holds a black belt in Shorin Ryu and Aikijujutsu.

Contenders

37 **"Calmness of Mind":** Shunryu Suzuki Roshi, *Not Always So* (HarperCollins, 2002), 5-7.

An Appropriate Response

41 **solitary visionary:** Norman Fischer, *Taking our Places: The Buddhist Path to Truly Growing Up* (HarperCollins, 2003), 9-10.

42 **it all depends:** Elizabeth Bishop, "It All Depends," *Mid-Century American Poets*, ed. John Ciardi (Twayne, 1950), 267.

43 **Imagine that you will have**: Phillip Moffitt, "The Heart's Intention," *The Best Buddhist Writing 2004*, ed. Melvin McLeod (Shambhala, 2004), 136-37.

44 **If you want the tree**: James Forest, "Nhat Hanh: Seeing with the Eyes of Compassion," in Thich Nhat Hanh, *The Miracle of Mindfulness* (Beacon, 1976), 103.

The Backward Step

46 **Stop searching**: Eihei Dogen, *Beyond Thinking*, ed. Kazuaki Tanahashi (Shambhala, 2004), 4. Translation by Edward Brown and the Editor.

Inhabiting Zen

49 **has always meant inhabiting**: James H. Austin, *Zen and the Brain* (MIT Press, 1998), 644.

50 **For a sentient being**: Tenshin Reb Anderson, *Being Upright: Zen Meditation and the Bodhisattva Precepts* (Rodmell Press, 2000), Kindle edition, 75-76.

51 **frozen blockage**: Menzan Zuiho Zenji, "Jijuyu-zanmai" ("Samadhi of the Self") in *Shikantaza: An Introduction to Zazen*, edited and translated by Shohaku Okumura (Kyoto Soto-Zen Center, 1985), 106.

52 **participate with the whole universe**: Shohaku Okumura, *Realizing Genjokoan* (Wisdom, 2010), Kindle edition, 70-71.

When the Horse-master: Shunryu Suzuki Roshi, *Zen Mind, Beginner's Mind* (Weatherhill, 1970), 81.

A Life's Work

53 John De Haan (1925-2008) directed the Clinton High School A Capella Choir in Clinton, Iowa for thirty-nine years.

Being Positive

58 **Is it just that humans**: Joan Sutherland, "The Whole Way," *The Best Buddhist Writing 2010*, ed. Melvin McLeod (Shambhala, 2011), Kindle edition, 25.

In the Waiting Room

62 **numberless beings**: Roshi Joan Halifax, *Upaya Zen Center Newsletter*, June 18, 2008.

see through the universal illusion: Alan Watts, *The Way of Zen*, Kindle edition, 2260.

63 **Hospitals are houses**: *Upaya Zen Center Newsletter*, June 23, 2008.

The Music of What Happens

64 Saigyo, *Poems of a Mountain Home*, tr. by Burton Watson (Columbia, 1991), 79.

65 Lafcadio Hearn, *Exotics and Retrospectives*, in Lafcadio Hearn, Elizabeth Bisland, *The Writings of Lafcadio Hearn* (Macmillan, 1922), 62.

Seamus Heaney, *Field Work* (Farrar, Straus, Giroux, 1979), 56.

66 Edward Hoagland, "Small Silences," *Sex and the River Styx* (Chelsea Green, 2011), 29.

Dramatis Personae

68 **Man is least himself**: Oscar Wilde, *The Critic as Artist: With Some Remarks Upon the Importance of Doing Nothing and Discussing Everything*.
See http://www.online-literature.com wilde/1305/

70 Ben Howard, *Midcentury* (Salmon Poetry, 1997). Patrick Chapman's review may be read at http://www.salmonpoetry.com/

Contemplative Memory

73 **And suddenly there's this feeling**: Sven Birkerts, *The Other Walk: Essays* (Graywolf, 2011), 114-115.

contemplative memory: Henri Bergson, *Matter and Memory* (Zone Books, 1988), Kindle edition, 201.

75 **Even in Kyoto**: Matsuo Basho, *Narrow Road to the Interior and Other Writings*, edited and translated by Sam Hamill (Shambhala, 1998), 155.

The Virtues of Solitude

76 **There is this cave**: James Wright, *Collected Poems* (Wesleyan University Press, 1971), 114.

77 **part of the discourse**: Sherry Turkle, *Alone Together* (Basic Books, 2011), Kindle edition, 296.

78 **Aware of my stability**: Thich Nhat Hanh, *The Blooming of a Lotus* (Beacon, 1993), 18-20.

does't do—it allows: Elizabeth Mattis-Namgyel, "The Power of an Open Question," *The Best Buddhist Writing 2011*, ed. Melvin McLeod (Shambhala, 2011), 139.

The Elbow Does Not Bend Outward

82 **A healthy information diet**: Clay Johnson, "Does Going On an Information Diet Improve One's Productivity?" http://www.quora.com/

one hundred per cent: Atul Gawande, "Letting Go," *The New Yorker*, July 26, 2010.

flunked hospice twice: Rev. Myo Lahey, Ash Interment Ceremony, June 26, 2004, http://www.archive.org/details/HSZC2004-06-26_Rev.Myo_Lahey_DharmaTalk.

Fresh Listening

84 **Can there be fresh speaking**: Toni Packer, *The Work of This Moment* (Tuttle, 1995), 1.

87 **the product of an unnatural marriage**: Elizabeth Poston, *The Penguin Book of Christmas Carols* (London: Penguin, 1965).

Westminster Cathedral Choir: http://www.youtube.com/watch?v=Gk3VMIJ7zSA

The Practice of Peace

88 Thich Nhat Hanh, *Calming the Fearful Mind: A Zen Response to Terrorism* (Parallax, 2005), 63. Subsequent quotations are also from this text.

91 Thich Nhat Hanh's retreat was entitled "Leading with Courage and Compassion."

Seventy Percent

93 **striving for 100 percent**: Bruce Frantzis, *The Big Book of Tai Chi* (Thorsons, 2003), 36.

can use your full effort: Frantzis, 191.

94 **Just as we should not idealize**: Grace Schireson, *Zen Women* (Wisdom, 2009), 250.

95 **becoming heroes**: Bruce Frantzis, *Opening the Energy Gates of Your Body* (North Atlantic Books, 1993), 85.

Paying Heed

98 **Ignoring the countless sights**: Jan Chozen Bays, *How to Train a Wild Elephant* (Shambhala, 2011), Kindle edition, 151.

The Ego Filter

101 *When we look out the window*: Shodo Harada Roshi, *Moon by the Window* (Wisdom, 2011), 21.

102 **root of the mind**: Reginald H. Pawle, "The Psychology of Zen Buddhism: Possibilities for Western Psychotherapy," *Japanese Journal of Psychotherapy*, vol. 30, no. 1 (February, 2004), 17-23.

Consistency

106 **Zen thought**: Reginald H. Pawle, "The Psychology of Zen Buddhism: Possibilities for Western Psychotherapy," *Japanese Journal of Psychotherapy*, vol. 30, no. 1 (February, 2004), 17-23.

Quiet Persistence

109 **Soft power is not limited**: Susan Cain, *Quiet: The Power of Introverts in a World That Can't Stop Talking* (Crown, 2012), Kindle edition, 200.

to embrace the power of quiet: Cain, 202.

110 **Inclusiveness is the capacity**: Thich Nhat Hanh, *The Heart of the Buddha's Teaching* (Parallax, 1998), 185, 189.

Wait Up!

113 **"We have to learn the art"**: Thich Nhat Hanh, *The Heart of the Buddha's Teaching* (Parallax, 1998), 23 .

Timeless Flowers

117 **Hana ni somu**: Saigyo, *Poems of a Mountain Home*, tr. Burton Watson (Columbia University Press, 1991), 39.

118 **When we were children**: Louis MacNeice, *Selected Poems*, ed. W.H. Auden (Faber, 1964), 80.

119 **"A Private History of Awe"**: Scott Russell Sanders, *Earth Works: Selected Essays* (Indiana University Press, 2012), 253-263.

"I must become a child again" is the closing line of Thomas Traherne's poem "Innocence."

Fixed Ideas

121 **release our idea of happiness**: Thich Nhat Hanh, "Cooling the Flames of Anger," Dharma talk, Dublin, Ireland, April 11, 2012.
http://tnhaudio.org/2012/04/18/cooling-the-flames-in-dublin/

Ezra Bayda, *Beyond Happiness* (Shambhala, 2011), Kindle edition, 2060, 2089, 849.

Watch What You're Doing

127 **in samadhi every moment**: Katsuki Sekida, *Two Zen Classics: Mumonkan and Hekiganroku* (Weatherhill, 1977), 45.

Mudita and Social Media

130 **multiplies in ratio**: C.F. Knight, "Mudita," in *Mudita: The Buddha's Teaching on Unselfish Joy*. Access to Insight.
http://www.accesstoinsight.org

It is relatively easier: Nyanaponika Thera, "Is Unselfish Joy Practicable?," *ibid*.

a depressing fact: Natasha Jackson, "Unselfish Joy: A Neglected Virtue," *ibid*.

131 **We all behold with envious eyes**: Jonathan Swift, "Verses on the Death of Dr. Swift," *The Writings of Jonathan Swift*, ed. Robert A. Greenberg and William B. Piper (Norton, 1973), 553. Spelling modernized.

132 **looking at things together**: Alexander made this remark while moderating a panel on the future of social media at the National Archives, Washington, D.C., November 21, 2011.

The Cliché Monster

135 **Nothing lasts**: Zoketsu Norman Fischer, "Impermanence is Buddha Nature," *Shambhala Sun* (May 2012), 50.

136 **snatch out of time**: Patrick Kavanagh, "The Hospital."

Just Say "Oh"

138 *To see the world*: Alan Watts, *The Way of Zen* (Vintage, 1957), Kindle edition, 3028.

139 **The Way**: Seng-ts'an, *Hsin-hsin Ming: Verses on the Faith-Mind*, trans. Richard B. Clarke.
http://www.mendosa.com/way.html

Holiness: Thich Nhat Hanh, *Nothing to Do, Nowhere to Go* (Parallax, 2007), 122.

To be honest: Wiltold Pilecki, *The Auschwitz Volunteer* (Aquila Polonica, 2012). Quoted by Timothy Snyder in his review "Were We All People?" *New York Times Book Review*, 6-22-12.

140 **Even brief silence**: George Prochnik, *In Pursuit of Silence* (Doubleday, 2011), Kindle edition, 49.

Noble Silence

141 **Another church**: Philip Larkin, *Collected Poems* (Farrar, Straus, Giroux, 1988), 97.

142 **soundscapes**: George Prochnik, *In Pursuit of Silence* (Doubleday, 2011), Kindle edition, 82.

epidemic of excessive: Prochnik, 235.

defiantly on the rise: Prochnik, 289.

144 **All formations are impermanent**: Thich Nhat Hanh, "This Silence is Called Great Joy," *Shambhala Sun*, September, 2007.

This World Uncertain Is

146 **Hertz's remark**: Loren Eiseley, *The Unexpected Universe* (Harcourt Brace, 1969), 41.

147 **a way of horizontalizing**: Philip Kapleau Roshi, *The Three Pillars of Zen* (Beacon, 1965), 174.

How that went against my grain: Philip Kapleau Roshi, *Zen: Merging of East and West* (Anchor, 1989), 191.

When entered into sincerely: *ibid.*, 192.

True Equanimity

149 **a mindful approach**: BOSU Fitness website. http://www.bosufitness.com/

150 **Upeksha means equanimity**: Thich Nhat Hanh, *The Heart of the Buddha's Teaching* (Parallax, 1998), 161-162.

151 **May I dwell: Pema Chodron**, *Comfortable with Uncertainty* (Shambhala, 2002), 78.

fully present: Zoketsu Norman Fischer, "Equanimity." Everyday Zen Foundation. http://www.everydayzen.org

152 **a state of inner equipoise**: Bhikkhu Bodhi, "Toward a Threshold of Understanding." Access to Insight. http://www.accesstoinsight.org

Resting in the Immediate

153 **This is some sort of duck**: Donald C. Babcock, "The Little Duck," *The New Yorker*, October 4, 1947. This poem also appears, slightly revised, in Donald C. Babcock's collection *New England Harvest* (Indiana University Press, 1953). The last line of the excerpt above becomes, "He has poise, however, and philosophers can use that."

154 **I spent years just trying**: Stefan Laeng-Gilliatt, "What Should We Be Tasting Now," interview with Edward Espe Brown, Charlotte Selver Oral History and Book Project. http://www.charlotteselverbook.org/Pages/Ed%20Brown.html

Our human nature: Roshi Pat Enkyo O'Hara,"The Identity of Relative and Absolute," *True Expression: Village Zendo Newsletter*, May, 2007.

This Is, Because That Is

158 **Buddhist genesis**: Thich Nhat Hanh, *The Heart of the Buddha's Teaching* (Parallax, 1998), 206.

159 **It's a little bit like a snowstorm**: Christina Feldman, "Dependent Origination."

Dropping and Adding

162 **Sometimes people say**: Toni Packer, *The Wonder of Presence* (Shambhala, 2002), 134.

163 **because the brain**: Charles Duhigg, *The Power of Habit* (Random House, 2012), Kindle edition, location 449.

encoded in the structures: Duhigg, 466.

Realizing

169 **Here is what I do**: Khaled Hosseini, *The Kite Runner* (Riverhead, 2003), 48.

170 **to render them real**: Drew Gilpin Faust, *This Republic of Suffering: Death and the American Civil War* (Knopf, 2008), Kindle edition, 2275.

The Handwritten Word

174 **we are at a moment**: Philip Hensher, "Why Handwriting Matters," *The Guardian*, October 6, 2012.

175 **Look, they say**: These lines appear in Sylvia Townsend Warner's review of Katherine Mansfield's letters. Warner's remarks are quoted by Claire Harman in her review of *With the Hunted*, a selection of Warner's writings, *Times Literary Supplement*, October 5, 2012, 4.

I wasn't really a writer: Patrick Kavanagh, *The Green Fool* (Penguin, 1971), 239.

Wise Attention

179 **wise attention**: Jack Kornfield, "A Mind Like Sky," *The Best Buddhist Writing 2004*, ed. Melvin McLeod (Shambhala, 2004), 329-334.

inner sound: Ajahn Amaro, "The Sound of Silence," *Buddhadharma*, Winter 2012, 27-31.

Snow

181 **crooked**: Friederike Boissevain, "Here With You," *Buddhadharma*, Winter 2012, 63.

184 **The snow falls**: Hayden Carruth, *Doctor Jazz* (Copper Canyon Press, 2001), 94.

Unwelcome Sounds

186 **Just imagine**: Roshi Pat Enkyo O'Hara, "Include Everything," *Shambhala Sun*, November 2012, 61.

188 **In this world**: Seng-ts'an, "Verses on the Faith-Mind," tr. Richard B. Clarke.

remain in the flow: Tilopa, "Song of the Mahamudra (Tilopa's song to Naropa).

Past and Present

190 **Irish taste buds**: Dennis O' Driscoll, *Reality Check* (Copper Canyon, 2008), 9-10.

191 **To conceive of 'now'**: Chris Arthur, *On the Shoreline of Knowledge* (University of Iowa Press, 2012), 118.

192 **The present contains the past**: Thich Nhat Hanh, *Our Appointment with Life* (Parallax, 1990), 32-33.

Elsewhere

197 **we were all through**: Richard Russo, *Nobody's Fool* (Vintage, 1993), 81.

lost in some labyrinth: Russo, *Elsewhere* (Knopf, 2012), 84.

198 Matthew A. Killingsworth and Daniel T. Gilbert, "A Wandering Mind is an Unhappy Mind," *Science*, vol. 330 (12 November 2010), 932.

About the Author

Poet and essayist Ben Howard was born in 1944 and grew up in eastern Iowa. His interest in Buddhist meditation originated in the 1970s, kindled by the prose of Peter Matthiessen and the poems of Gary Snyder. Having learned the fundamentals of sitting practice from Allen Ginsberg in 1978, he became a student of Vipassana meditation and later of Vietnamese Rinzai Zen, as taught by the Venerable Thich Nhat Hanh. More recently, he has studied Japanese Rinzai Zen with Jiro Osho Fernando Afable and Shinge Roko Sherry Chayat Roshi. In 2002 he received the jukai precepts in the Hakuin/Torei lineage of Rinzai Zen at Dai Bosatsu Zendo.

Howard holds a doctorate in English Literature from Syracuse University, where he studied with Donald Justice, Philip Booth, and William Wasserstrom. Before his retirement in 2006, he taught literature, writing, classical guitar, and Buddhist meditation at Alfred University. Over the past four decades he has contributed poems, essays, articles, and reviews to literary journals here and abroad, including *Poetry*, the *Sewanee Review*, *Poetry Ireland Review*, and *Shenandoah*. The author of nine books, he has been the recipient of numerous awards, including the Milton Dorfman Prize in Poetry and a fellowship from the National Endowment for the Arts. He lives with his wife, Robin Caster Howard, in the village of Alfred, New York.

Praise for *Entering Zen*

Howard has written a refreshingly unpretentious, down-home account of the practice of Zen. He warns of the danger of naming things, yet offers a clear-eyed investigation into how language can, indeed, express the ineffable. He illuminates personal epiphanies in a way that brings us fully into the realm of pure experience, beyond duality.

— Shinge Roko Sherry Chayat Roshi, Abbot, Dai Bosatsu Zendo and Zen Center of Syracuse

This wise volume of essays by writer and Zen practitioner Ben Howard is a powerful invitation to stop and look deeply into one's life and see below the surface into its great potential. A book for those who practice meditation, it is also an adventure for those who don't; the beauty of the writing and the delight of the insights our author shares with us are enriching and surprising. This is one of those literary treasures that will become a classic in its time.

— Roshi Joan Halifax. Abbot, Upaya Zen Center, and author of *Being with Dying*

Poet and critic Ben Howard shows us, in seventy-five essays about a thousand words each, how to learn to perceive the passing moment as the immediate entry into deeper awareness. He eschews sentimentality, avoids bromides, and shares compassion. . . . Without any pretension, but with careful prose and a subtle poetic skill, Howard reminds me here of what I first encountered (years before) in his essays on Irish writing "The Pressed Melodeon" and more recently in his "Leaf, Sunlight, Asphalt" (2009) verses: the calm, recollected power of tranquility amidst energy.

— John L. Murphy, Amazon Top 500 Reviewer

[O]rder a copy of Entering Zen *and discover a work of depth and subtlety. You might also add Ben's blog to your RSS reader. There are many Buddhist blogs active today, but you won't find any of greater depth than One Time, One Meeting.*

— Barry Briggs, Dharma Master in the Kwan Um School of Zen

Each essay cuts right to the living heart of Zen. Howard guides us as a spiritual friend -- wise, knowledgeable (without ever being pedantic), kind-hearted and witty. These finely wrought essays reflect decades of work toiling in poetic vineyards -- they are the epitome of grace and transparency.

— Seth Segall, *The Existential Buddhist*

These 75 essays offer teachings on Zen that show the practice as basic yet intricate, ordinary yet elegant. To shine these jewels of practice, Howard draws from his immense knowledge and wisdom of literature, poetry, Buddhist practice, and an intimacy with his own life.

— Lynette Monteiro, *108 Zen Books*

Entering Zen is available from amazon.com and other online booksellers. ISBN: 978-0-9770956-7-4

www.ingramcontent.com/pod-product-compliance
Lightning Source LLC
Chambersburg PA
CBHW051648040426
42446CB00009B/1029